Afternoon.

2.0 — 2.40	2.0 / 2.15	2.40 — 3.20	3.20 / 3.30	3.30 — 4.0	4.0 — 4.30	
Private Study Drawing.		History		(A) French (B) Reading	Music.	
— do —		— do —		— do —	do.	
— do —		— do —		Drill or Rea...	...or Drill	
— do. —		Music			...ading	
(A) French (B) Writing	Register closed 2.15	Map Drawing			Reading	
Map Drawing		(A) French (B) Writing		Woodwork	— do. —	
Composition.		Reading		Recitation.	Recitation.	
Geography.		Physical Exercise		(A) French (B) Reading	Writing	
Science Lesson.		— do. —		Reading	(A) French (B) Writing	
Mathematics		Geography	Recreation.	Recitation.	Music	Dismissal.
— do. —		History.		— do. —	— do. —	
— do. — Cookery	First Roll 2.	Composition.		— do. —	Drawing.	
Map Drawing Woodwork		Writing. Laundry do.		Music and Reading.	Reading Writing.	
Arithmetic				Housewifery.		
Boys. — Art		Class ; 2-3				
Girls. Needle[work]		work 3.30-4.30		Physical Exercises 3-3.30		
Science Lesson.		Map Drawing		Music	Reading	
Drawing		Recitation		Geography	(A) French (B) Reading	
— do. —		Music		— do. —	— do. —	
Private Study		Boys Physical Exercises / Girls Talks on Morals		(A) French (B) Reading	Discussion on Events of the Week.	
— do. — & Drawing				— do. —		
Drawing		Reading		Music		
Boys. Writing		Reading		Organised Games.		
Girls. Needlework. Woodwork 2-3. 3.30-4.30				Physical Exercises 3-3.30		

One hundred years of London education 1870-1970

Stuart Maclure

Allen Lane The Penguin Press

Copyright © Stuart Maclure, 1970

First published in 1970

Allen Lane The Penguin Press
Vigo Street, London W1

ISBN 0 7139 0176 4

Printed in Great Britain by
The Whitefriars Press Ltd
London and Tonbridge

Contents

List of illustrations

7

New approaches to language teaching included gramophone records and visual aids – Balham Central School, 1935.
Group music instruction at Catford Central School, 1936.
Old Castle Street School, Whitechapel, the first school opened by the London School Board, 1873.
Thirty years later, the London three-decker style had been established as, here, at John Ruskin School, Camberwell.
Thirty years later still, in a more open style, Ealdham Square School gives each class room access to the playground.
The recreational side of the evening institutes continued to flourish and new subjects were added to the list of courses as, for example, beauty-culture at Barnett Street Evening Institute, 1936.
Domestic-science teaching showed the kind of household equipment which girls were expected to use in later life – the laundry class at Carlyle School, 1938.
An after-care conference at Durham Hill School, 1937.
The care committee workers formed the nucleus of a welfare staff. Here a welfare inspector makes a call in Hoxton, 1939.
Part of an exhibition of students' work at Charing Cross Underground station designed to show the public the range of activities at the evening institutes, 1936.
A cartoon by Grimes used in a big advertising campaign in the summer of 1939, ready for the opening of the autumn term.

following page 160:

Group work within a single class enables children to get on with their own chosen work. Middle Row Primary School, 1969.
Split-level class room at the Vittoria School, Islington. (*The Times*)
A scene at a London railway station a few days before the outbreak of the Second World War. A party of London elementary-school children set off for the country. (*Radio Times Hulton Picture Library*)
Part of a letter by a girl evacuated with Camden High School to Uppingham. (*Camden High School*)
Practical work can include domestic science for boys: a cookery exercise for boys at Gipsy Road Elementary School, 1942. (*Radio Times Hulton Picture Library*)
Third-formers in the brickwork shop at a technical institute. (*The Times*)
In the machine shop at Eltham Green School, Woolwich, 1956. (*Radio Times Hulton Picture Library*)
Sixth-form biology at Sir Walter St John's School, 1962.
A child at Gateforth Primary School, 1964, explains the theory and practice of school meals.
Children at the Gateway Primary School, 1963, sitting down to 'family service', six to a table.
New approaches to number teaching – many of them as old as the London School Board – involve the children in measuring and weighing everyday objects as here at Normand Park School, 1962.
Early designs like Kidbrooke, 1954, produced massive buildings for 1,800–2,000 pupils. (*Aerofilms Ltd*)
Morning assembly at Archway School, 1965.
A typical primary-school scene – the nature table at Danebury Primary School, 1959.
Shallow learner-pools like this at Middle Row Primary School, 1969, give all children the chance to learn to swim.
Concentrated activity in craft work at Stockwell Primary School, 1967.

Working in the school flat at Tollington Park, 1963.
Supermarket skills at Hammersmith County School for Girls, 1968.
Girls on a commercial course at the South Eastern College of Further Education, 1969, learn to use modern office equipment.
Lord Boyle, then Parliamentary Secretary at the Ministry of Education, with children at the Franklin D. Roosevelt School for physically handicapped children, 1957. (*Sport and General*)
Using powerful amplifying equipment to teach deaf boys and girls at the Oak Lodge Special School, 1969.
Drama and music bring a response from children at Wycliffe Special School (educationally subnormal), 1969.
Northern Polytechnic is one of the colleges which have shared in the expansion of advanced work in technology.
A primary school teacher presents a programme at the formal opening of the I.L.E.A. educational TV studios in Islington. (*The Times*)

Line Illustrations

All illustrations except those credited otherwise have been supplied by the Greate London Council.

Preface

This book originated in an invitation by Sir William Houghton, education officer of the Inner London Education Authority, to prepare a 'short history' of London education in the 100 years following the 1870 Education Act. I say 'short history' advisedly because it would require far greater resources than I possess in scholarship and time to attempt the major task which has still to be tackled. It is one thing to skim the surface of the records in the archives at County Hall: it would be quite another to write the definitive work.

There is another important limitation to the scope of this study which should be noted. It is mainly concerned with those aspects of education in London which came within the responsibility and influence of the London School Board, the London ounty Council Education Committee and the Inner London Education Authority. This means it has little to say about the Church elementary schools, before 1904, little to say about secondary schools before 1904, little to say about university education. The author may be grateful for these exclusions but should make the fact known to the reader at the outset.

The story is one of rapid and continuous development: the Education Act of 1870 was the first step which, once taken, led on progressively to a wider and deeper involvement. Initially the public education system was restricted to the lower social classes and the lower sub-teen age-groups. Decade by decade the level of participation rose, both in terms of social class and the age-range. What began as a limited experiment in elementary education became a comprehensive system of education from the nursery school to the university: and in so far as this statement immediately exposes the fact that the system is still incomplete, it shows that this process of development and expansion must still continue after a century's work.

In the first heroic thirty-four years, the London School Board – a body which it is only possible to hold in the highest admiration – established the

A*

main lines of an elementary system. In the higher grade schools there were the seeds of something more. In the later years, the Technical Education Board, working alongside and sometimes in rivalry with the School Board, prepared the way for the new education authority after 1904 to take up responsibilities for secondary and higher education.

The vitality continued to 1914 in the ten crowded years in which Blair refashioned the separate elements into a new working system – a system which continued in all its essentials through the period between the wars. 'Secondary education for all' became the dominant theme and a series of studies and reports between 1926 and 1939 show how this came to be crystallized in London into the idea of the comprehensive school. Finally, the third part of this account seeks briefly to sketch the way in which, since 1945, London's education system has exploded, how it has grown in size, but more importantly also how the aims and aspirations which it expresses have expanded.

I would like to put on record the help I have received from many quarters: from the I.L.E.A., notably from Sir William Houghton, the education officer, and from Mr R. M. Gordon, assistant education officer, and the patient staff of the record room and libraries at County Hall. In particular I am indebted to Mr W. H. Milner for the bibliography at the back of this book.

I must also acknowledge the help I have received from Mr David Allsobrook, who acted as a research assistant; Mr Peter Scott and Mr Martin Shepherd; Mr Arthur Lockwood, who worked on the pictures; and Miss Victoria Broad who typed the manuscript and, of course, my wife who also worked on the pictures and helped me at every stage.

Part one *1870-1904*

1 *Laying the foundations*

London went to the polls for the first time to elect an education authority – the London School Board – on Tuesday, 29 November 1870. The excitement was considerable – the atmosphere almost euphoric. The Elementary Education Act, which had gone through Parliament earlier in the year, driven through by Mr Gladstone himself and by its author, Mr W. E. Forster, vice-president of the Committee of Council, had been a great controversial measure. Repeated attempts to put an elementary education act on the statute book had, during the previous forty years, failed because of the opposition of the Church of England to state intervention and the opposition of the non-conformists and radicals to a clerical monopoly. Throughout the debates at Westminster the religious issues dominated the discussion. But alongside them, and eventually outweighing them, was the growing recognition of the scale of educational destitution, particularly in the great cities.

The precise figures are open to question – the statistics were anything but reliable – but the physical evidence from all the big towns was available for all to see. Between a half and a quarter of the children were out of school and voluntary effort was unable to do much more than keep up with the rise in population.

The task which Forster set himself was one which demanded consummate political tact and skill. He had to draft a Bill which would conjure up schools for the children who were not already provided for, without so affronting the ecclesiastical and other interests, which were committed to the voluntary schools, as to reduce the level of philanthropic activity.

If political necessity dictated a policy of 'filling up the gaps', so did economic sense. Forster could not afford to throw away the resources which were already being provided by the voluntary effort. And so, too, did the general opinion of respectable citizens of the time who were quite prepared to recognize a special position for the Churches in education, which accurately expressed the important position which moral training occupied among the limited aims of elementary education.

To understand the School Board period, it is necessary to note that elementary education was a term which defined a social pattern as well as an intellectual grade. Elementary education was explicitly concerned with the education of the lower classes, the sons and daughters of working men. Its minimum content had been narrowly prescribed by the codes of the Education Department. Government subsidies were only paid upon the examination of the children in carefully defined standards by Her Majesty's Inspectors and their assistants.

Public elementary schools were for the 'elementary school class' – a familiar descriptive term. Those who taught in them also came from within this category.

Alongside the system of elementary schools (and quite outside the 1870 Act) there were other schools for the various gradations of middle-class children. These included the 'public schools', narrowly interpreted as nine schools – Eton, Winchester, Westminster, Charterhouse, St Paul's, Merchant Taylors', Harrow, Rugby and Shrewsbury – and the Endowed Schools (including many of the old grammar schools which had just been reviewed by the Taunton Commission and whose charters and statutes were about to be revised by the Endowed School Commissioners). Although this sector constituted the nation's secondary schools, many of them had junior departments or schools of one kind or another which existed to feed them with pupils, and collectively this added up to a school system entirely separate from and parallel to that being set up for working-class children.

Between these middle-class schools of differing aspirations and the elementary schools was a rich variety of private schools of uneven quality, running from the small dame schools, which were little more than child-minding establishments, and schools run in miserable conditions by unqualified staff, to well-equipped and efficient schools aimed at educating future clerks and tradesmen. The rule of thumb which divided them was financial. A fee of less than 9*d.* a week put the school in the elementary school class; to charge more than that elevated the school to a more select social grade.

One reason why action to set up some public system of elementary schools had been so long delayed was the absence of any adequate units of local government capable of raising and administering local funds for schooling. Forster's original intention had been that the borough councils and parish vestries should nominate members to serve on the school boards which were to be set up to run the system. In the event, the Bill was amended and the boards were to be recruited by direct election, although the rate was to be raised by precept on the vestries.

As the election advertisements which appeared in *The Times* during the three months before the first election of the London School Board indicate, the religious issue dominated the elections – not in the advocacy of specific policies, so much as in the identification of candidates with one set of interests or the other.

Most of the candidates in 1870 made conventional election promises about economy and efficiency but few entered the election with any detailed policies for education. Party labels were unknown at first; later national party divisions were reflected on the Board where members stood as Progressives or Moderates.

If *The Times* is any reliable guide,* the electors had a remarkable awareness that they were making history. The school boards were more than instruments of educational administration. In the absence of major elected units of local government, they represented a bold experiment in democratic institutions.

London had only been brought under the 1870 Act by an afterthought. The original intention had been to deal with the metropolis in a later Bill, dividing the capital up into smaller units of administration based on the workhouse school districts and the vestry boundaries. In the event, the Commons carried an amendment put forward by Mr W. M. Torrens, M.P. for Finsbury (and a member of the first London School Board) – against the advice of Mr W. E. Forster – the effect of which was to bring London under the Bill and designate the 114 square miles of the area of the Metropolitan Board of Works as the jurisdiction of the London School Board.

London was divided into ten electoral divisions. Four of these returned four members each: City, Southwark, Chelsea and Greenwich. Four more – Lambeth, Tower Hamlets, Hackney and Westminster – were assigned

* 'The great event of today for this country, whatever may be happening on the Continent of Europe will be the election of the first London School Board. No equally powerful body will exist in England outside Parliament, if power be measured by influence for good or evil over masses of human beings.' (Leading article in *The Times*, 29 November 1870.) The events on the Continent of Europe which the leader writer had in mind, by way of contrast, included the siege of Paris and the repudiation by the Russians of the conditions laid down by Palmerston after the Crimean War, which limited Russian naval power in the Black Sea. It was less than three months since Napoleon III's army had been defeated at Sedan.

five members each. Finsbury was represented by six members and Marylebone by seven.*

Each elector could cast as many votes as there were seats in his division. The vote could be used cumulatively – the voter could 'plump' all his votes on a single candidate if he wished to, instead of spreading them through the list.

This enabled minorities to get their representative on. It also evoked fears that it would lead to the election of cranks and faddists, but these were unfounded. Another novelty was voting by secret ballot – anticipating the Ballot Act for parliamentary elections – except for the City of London.

One of the consequences of making the School Board an *ad hoc* authority, charged with the development of a single service, was that people who were specially interested in education, but might not otherwise have entered local politics, were prepared to stand for election. By common consent the quality of the candidates was high. The *Quarterly* commented on 'the high class of men who have become candidates and been elected'. In what must have been a sweeping judgement in advance of the evidence, the same writer divined that 'the electors have chosen men who put education first and economy second'. And not men only, of course. Another respect in which the school boards were breaking new ground was in allowing women to stand for election.

Two distinguished women were elected to the London School Board, the first of a long line of women board members and councillors who have played a notable part in London government. One was Miss Emily Davies, the other Dr Elizabeth Garrett (later Mrs Elizabeth Garrett Anderson), the first woman doctor. Dr Garrett topped the poll in Marylebone, receiving more votes than any other candidate in the whole election.

There was no shortage of talent. Thomas Gautrey, who was connected with the Board throughout its thirty-three-year life as teacher, union leader and member, wrote a series of entertaining thumb-nail sketches of some of the members whom he described collectively as 'liberal minded men and women filled with confidence and buoyant hopes'.

The Anglicans were there in strength – among them the Rev. W. H. Thorold (later Bishop of Rochester), Dr Barry, principal of King's College, London (later Bishop of Sydney) and Canon J. G. Cromwell, principal of St Mark's College ('I thank God I have never entered a Board school'). There were also powerful Anglican figures who were anything but

---

* In 1882, Chelsea was given an extra member. Later, Lambeth was split into two divisions: East Lambeth (four seats) and West Lambeth (six seats).

sectarian by temperament – among them the Rev. William ('Hang theology') Rogers, rector of St Botolph's, Bishopsgate, the Rev. John Rodgers, vicar of St Thomas, Charterhouse, and later, the Rev. Stewart Headlam who combined Christian Socialism with a passion for evening schools.

The Free Churches also had their spokesmen. Dr J. H. Rigg, principal of the Wesleyan Training College in Horseferry Road, Westminster, was a member of the first two boards. (His daughter, Edith Rigg, became the founder and headmistress for forty-one years of the Mary Datchelor Grammar School.) He was a Moderate and had more in common with the Anglicans – the Wesleyans still had many schools of their own – than with the extreme view which later came to be represented on the Board by such men as the Rev. William Hamilton (Baptist), the Rev. W. Copeland Bowie (Unitarian) and the Rev. John Sinclair (Congregationalist) who led the fight on behalf of non-conformity when Mr Athelstan Riley was campaigning against the religious compromise. The Roman Catholics did not contest the elections as a body but the cumulative vote used in School Board elections helped them – as it did later the teachers themselves – to ensure that their minority voice was heard. Colonel Lenox Prendergast sat for Tower Hamlets and often voted with the Progressives, while Father Beckley (also Tower Hamlets) and Father, later Bishop, W. F. Brown who represented Southwark, also gave firm support to the Progressives.

Among the politicians there were several M.P.s – Mr W. H. Smith, the future First Lord of the Admiralty immortalized by W. S. Gilbert; Mr Charles Reed (later Sir Charles), who became vice-chairman and later chairman of the Board; Lord Sandford (afterwards Earl of Harrowby); Mr Samuel Morley and Mr W. M. Torrens – the 'father of the Board'.

It was on 15 December 1870 that the London School Board met for the first time at Guildhall (by invitation of the City). All but one of the elected members were present. Mr Torrens took the chair for the first item of business – the election of the first chairman of the Board.

But before they could elect a chairman, the members had to decide whether to use the power given to London under the Education Act to pay him a salary.* Professor Huxley and Mr Lucraft proposed and seconded a motion that no salary should be paid. This was carried by a majority with Lord Lawrence, who was shortly afterwards voted into the chair, among the minority.

* Payment for the chairman was again proposed and rejected in 1879 and 1880, when a motion to pay a salary of £1,500 a year was rejected by 30 to 3.

Lord Lawrence was an able administrator, recently returned from India where he had served as Viceroy, who gave general support to the Liberals in the House of Lords. He had been the first Indian civilian administrator to hold the highest office in the Empire since Warren Hastings, and his period of office immediately followed the Mutiny. According to the *Dictionary of National Biography*, he did not introduce any sweeping reforms but 'sanitation, both military and municipal, irrigation, railway extension and peace' had been his chief aims – an interesting combination of the general and the particular.

He was a popular and respected chairman. Someone with his national reputation was needed to lead a body which contained so many formidable members. He was described as 'rough and unconventional in manners' and 'as negligent and unconventional in his dress as he was in his words and bearing' – an unusual quality in a former Viceroy. For a time he had been at Clifton as a day boy – an unhappy time, as he remembered: 'I was flogged once every day of my life at school except one, and then I was flogged twice'. (One of the characteristics of the L.S.B. was to be that it was consistently less inclined towards corporal punishment than its teachers.)

Temporary accommodation was rented in New Bridge Street, near Ludgate Circus, for three years at £200 a year, until the Board could move into a building (since demolished) which stood near where the statue of W. E. Forster now stands in the Embankment Gardens.

The Board had to set up an administration from scratch with £25 in the petty cash. The first appointments were advertised and there were eighty-nine applicants for the top job as clerk with a salary of £800 a year (Huxley had tried to make it £1,000).

The successful candidate was George Hector Croad, a Cambridge graduate who had taught at Rossall school for ten years before leaving teaching to become an administrator. At the time of his appointment he was secretary of the Bishop of London's Fund. At 42, he was an efficient manager but in no sense a director of education or the Board's educational adviser. This was not a function which the Board recognized. Croad – 'a typical Civil Servant', 'tall, monocled, spruce, well dressed and courteous, but modest and retiring' – held office for almost the whole of the period of the Board's existence, retiring in 1902 on grounds of ill health.

Other senior officials to be appointed during the early months included Mr Isitt, statistical clerk (£350 a year); Mr G. A. Attenborough, finance clerk (£250); Mr Thomas Smith, head master of Hampden Gurney

Church of England School, Marylebone, who became first clerk to the all-important School Management Committee, and Mr Thomas Alfred Spalding, secretary to the Chairman throughout the life of the Board (£300), who wrote a highly informative record of the Board's work in 1900 on the occasion of the Paris exhibition. An ex-guardsman, Basson by name (25s. a week), was engaged as messenger.

The London Board was dominated for most of its thirty-odd years of life by the Progressive Party which coincided – very imperfectly – with Liberals at Westminster. At the beginning politics were not particularly important – though the atmosphere was often contentious and the Board seemed ready to vote at the drop of a hat on any and every topic. It was said that many of the first members belonged to the 'policy of the Board' party – they went along with the balance of opinion as the Board began to set up an administration.

As the clerical interest was inclined to object to any activity on the part of the Board which raised the standards by which Church schools could be judged (and therefore the cost which the Churches would have to pay to keep up) the clerical opposition attacked the Board's 'extravagance' and formed a natural alliance with the 'economists' – rate-payers' representatives and those whose general political sympathies, mainly Tory, were in favour of keeping taxes down and supporting the Church. In terms of London School Board politics, this was the alliance which formed the Moderates who contested the School Board elections from 1873 onwards and who swept into power in 1885 under the leadership of the Rev. J. R. Diggle.

Mr Diggle was a stern disciplinarian who sharpened the party battle and took care to see his supporters were in a majority on all important committees. His strong and abrasive personality led to the personalizing of many issues – 'Diggleism' was the subject of concerted attacks from the Progressive side and drew early fire from the Fabians who interested themselves in the London School Board in the 1890s. Diggleism came to be equated with meanness and illiberalism but, as it happened, the period of Moderate rule coincided with a surge forward as the fruits of the earlier work became apparent and there is a sense in which the Diggle thunder against extravagance eased, rather than hindered this.

In 1894 the Moderates gained a narrow majority but were split over the leadership and Mr Diggle had lost the support he needed if he was to continue as chairman. For the last ten years of its life, the Board had independent chairmen from outside. The first was Lord George Hamilton, who left after eight months to take up a Government appointment, followed by Lord Londonderry, who entertained Board members, chief officers and London teachers lavishly at Londonderry House and thereby helped to restore some of the geniality which had disappeared during the last years of Diggleism. The last chairman was an ex-Governor of Bombay, the distinguished and cultivated Lord Reay.

One of those who contributed most to the work of the Board – and one of its most distinctive and potent personalities – was the Hon. Lyulph Stanley, later Lord Sheffield, who represented Marylebone from 1876 to 1888 and from 1891 to 1904. Stanley was an agnostic free-thinker who, as his nephew, Bertrand Russell, put it, 'spent his time fighting the Church on the London School Board' – a not altogether adequate assessment because his total devotion to London education rose above his religious prejudices and this was so transparent that he was able to induce several influential members who differed from him on many matters to work with him on common education policies – notably General Moberly and even Thomas Huggett who, in spite of his dedication to the reduction of School Board expenditure, was persuaded to help with expert personal advice on school sites and buildings.

In manner he was brusque and direct with a keen intellect and a shrewd intelligence. He was an ex-fellow of Balliol and a friend of Jowett, with all the aristocratic confidence and authority which his background gave him. His family was notorious for an eccentric strain, which took his elder brother to the East where he became a Moslem while another of his brothers went over to Rome, becoming a bishop and chaplain to the Pope. His own eccentricity was elementary education and the welfare of London's children. To this he applied himself single-mindedly, and, aided by twenty-five years' experience and an excellent memory, became an authority on every aspect of the Board's activities. It was he who led the School Board's defence against the encroachments of the Technical Education Board. Like a number of other members, he combined School Board membership with active philanthropy, maintaining a private fund to help pay the training college fees of poor pupil teachers, and to help other protégées. He once caused some embarrassment by befriending the daughter of the school keeper at a school in North London of which he was a manager and inviting her parents to allow her to stay at his country house during school holidays.

There was no lack of interesting personalities among those who served on the Board, and any attempt to list them briefly is liable to turn into an uninformative catalogue. There were some strangely assorted characters. Mrs Annie Besant spent a brief period on the Board from 1888 to 1891. Her particular interest was to ensure that the Board's building contracts included a water-tight clause requiring the contractor to pay full union rates. She did her homework and proved an effective member, till, under the influence of Madame Blavatsky, she became more interested in theosophy than trade unionism.

For the first twenty years, one of the members for Finsbury was Benjamin Lucraft, an old Chartist, a cabinet maker by trade. He had strong ideas about curriculum, being eager that education should be made attractive. He was hotly opposed to corporal punishment.

Altogether some 302 men and twenty-four women sat on the London School Board during its thirty-four years of life. Half of them served for only a single three-year session. The School Board had a job to do unlike that ever tackled before by any other elected body and clearly the members relished it. Each member was linked directly with the schools in the division which he was elected to represent.

The school log books throughout the period make it clear that the Member of the Board was a figure of great prestige who kept a close eye on his 'own' schools – calling in from time to time to 'prove' the register (that is, make sure the head was not artificially inflating his numbers) and serving on many managing bodies. Many members devoted most of their time to the Board, visiting schools, attending committees, sub-committees and managers' meetings. As one who taught in London under the School Board put it: 'as there were seven times as many Board members as there were Board Inspectors, the local member was a much more familiar figure in the schools than the local inspector'.

Later this came to be regarded as one of the distinguishing characteristics of this phase in London's school system – the personal relationships established between the Board and the schools – and, with the rosy view of retrospect, this became a golden age when the administration could be described as 'democratic' in contrast to the 'bureaucratic' professional administration introduced later by the L.C.C.

2 First things first

The first task of the Board and its officers was to assess London's need for schools. Three weeks after the first meeting, a Statistical Committee was set up to whom fell the duty of preparing the returns called for by the Education Department in Circular 86, issued on 23 December 1870.

The circular called for a great deal of detail, much of which was never provided for London, but the main requirement was an estimate of the number of children in need of elementary education and the number of additional places required to provide for them. With splendid simplicity the Education Department asked for all the information within four months.

London's greatest difficulty was in tracking down and enumerating the children. Eventually after petitioning the Home Office for cooperation, the London School Board persuaded the Registrar General (much against his will) to provide copies of the census returns for 2 April 1871. Twelve months later, the Board was reporting to the Education Department that London's population was 3,265,005. Of these, 681,000 were children aged between 3 and 13, of whom 97,307 were being educated at home or attended schools charging fees of 9d. or more and were therefore not of the social class for whom elementary schools had to be provided.* A further 9,101 were 'inmates of institutions'. This left 574,693 children to be schooled.

Finding out what proportion of them were already in school and in schools of what quality, was the other half of the job. Here the inquiry techniques were far less satisfactory than for the census. The School Board set up local divisional committees, each with a superintendent and staff of enumerators. The agents had to fill in details of the teaching staff and their qualifications, if any, the dimensions of each school, the hours of opening, the ages and numbers of the children, the fees charged and the subjects taught.

On this basis it was calculated that 'of the children . . . belonging to the class which requires elementary schools' – numbering 574,693 – '398,679

* The purchasing power of 9d. per week in 1871 would amount over a forty-week school year to £12–£15 in 1970.

were attending and 176,014 for various causes were not attending school'.

The assessment was open to error because of the shifting population and because of the nature of many of the schools which children attended. The agents' task was often unpleasant as well as difficult, but great efforts were made to get all the schools listed in three categories – public, private and private adventure. The public elementary schools were those set up under a trust deed. Private schools were those conducted by committees of managers, but not under any deed of trust. Private adventure schools were commercial ventures.

There were two more calculations to be made. First of all, what proportion of the 574,693 children between 3 and 13 had to be provided for? Second, what proportion of the existing school places were suitable and efficient? To answer the first question, the statistical committee made a series of deductions from the original figure. There were those children under 5 whose parents refused to send them or who were regarded as too young – 55,760. Among the excuses given by the older non-attenders were illness (14,829), disablement (2,673), 'working at home' (9,816), 'working abroad', half-timers (1,332), whole-timers (27,045), absent from neglect or other causes (64,559).

The Board reckoned that, for all practical purposes, half the number absent for full-time work had to be allowed as reasonable, and similarly that half-timers only warranted half-accommodation in school. Many of the children aged 10 or over would claim full or partial exemption. On this basis, it was estimated that more than half the absentees – 95,975 – could be said to have valid excuses.

This reduced the number of putative places required to 478,718, from which the Board decided to deduct an arbitrary five per cent for other legitimate forms of temporary absence, bringing the final estimate for the number of children for whom places were required down to 454,783.

The Education Department, assessing the needs of the country as a whole, had evolved a rule of thumb which assumed the relevant child population to be one-sixth of the total all-age population. By this reckoning, London needed 540,000 school places. It was not surprising that, as the magnitude of the task of providing schools on that scale became apparent, the early School Boards should seek other less lavish bases for estimating the numbers. Subsequent School Boards moved the figures upwards and questioned the methods of the early Boards, in particular the extra five per cent deduction for temporary absence, and the failure to allow for the

1876 Laystall Street, Board School [1]
Aug 14 Boys' Department, opened this day
Admitted 72.
17 Mr Lovell visited the schools
23 Mr Groom visited the schools, also
Mr Pollock
24 A scholar named W Sargent was yester
day pushed down in the street by another
boy and his knee was cut. He told his
mother that the master had cut his knee
open with the cane. After school hours the
mother came and made a disturbance on the
school premises. This morning I sent for
the mother and after letting her hear from
witnesses a true account of the cut knee,
refused to receive the boy into the school
again till she had been before the managers
25 Revd A Fryer visited the schools
29 Mr Lovell visited the schools
30 Mr Groom visited the schools
Sep 5 Mr Ricks, Board Inspector, visited
the Schools
6 Mr Mark Wilks visited the
schools

Extract from an early log book.

rate of growth of the child population and the time lag between planning and provision.

As to the second question – the sufficiency and efficiency of the existing schools – the School Board sub-contracted the task of assessing the efficiency of the existing schools to the Education Department, who seconded H.M.I.s to carry out the necessary investigations. They concluded that there were 1,149 schools having places for 312,925 scholars which were 'efficient' and 250 schools which were partly efficient and capable of being adequately improved, which provided an additional 37,995 places, making a total of 350,920 places to set against an estimated need of 454,783, leaving a deficiency of 103,863 places to be provided.

It will be seen that, even using methods of calculation which clearly underestimated the extent of educational destitution, the Board came to the conclusion that two children in every nine were unprovided for. As things turned out, within twenty years London was providing as many places as the earlier Education Department estimate would have required – not just because the population had risen, but because of the success of the school attendance officers in getting hitherto unschooled social groups into school.

There can be little doubt that the early estimates were too low and that some of the schools which were accepted as efficient were very poor indeed. Dr E. G. West has suggested that, at the time of the 1870 Act, propagandists who wanted the state to intervene in education exaggerated the demand for places, and has offered his own more modest statistical assessments of need.* It is quite clear, however, that there was no disposition to do this in London and that later events vindicated those who believed that the early estimates were far too low. There is no lack of evidence of the poor quality of much which passed for schooling in the reports of the H.M.I.s published each year by the Education Department. To give one example of many –

Scott Naismith Stokes, H.M.I., reported on the schools of Southwark (in the Committee of Council's Report, 1872-3):

The following localities exhibit the most striking instances of deficiency:
A. The district adjoining Lambeth, and bounded by the Thames on the north, by Blackfriars Road in the east, and by the New Cut on the south, has 929 children requiring education and no efficient school existing or projected.
B. The larger and more populous tract lying between Union Street on the north and Blackman Street on the east, Suffolk Street on the south and

* *Education and the State*, I.E.A., 1965.

Blackfriars Road on the west, contains 2,739 children requiring new schools.

C. Between Horselydown and Great Dover Street live 1,759 children without schools.

D. Between Dock Head, Bermondsey and Cherry Gardens Pier 1,487 children need schools.

E. Between Hunter Street and Bermondsey New Road, 1,152 children are in the same plight.

F. Between Bermondsey Street and Dock Head live another neglected batch of 726.

G. Between Gloucester Road, Bermondsey and Jamaica Road the returns show a school deficiency for 3,295 children.

H. And between Paradise Row, Rotherhithe and the river, a further deficiency for 863 children. . . .

To meet the proved requirement for Southwark, the School Board for London propose to build schools for 11,200 . . . I trust that the new institutions will be numerous enough and so placed that young and timid children may have access to a school without crossing thronged thoroughfares, that ample space will be provided in them for girls and infants. . . .

Better in my opinion to leave them on the streets than to gather them in some of the places miscalled schools.

Evils do not tend to cure themselves by aggregation, and the mere collection of dirt and disorder is but the propagation of mischief.

The London School Board soon exceeded its own early estimate for school building need. By 1889 the number of places actually provided – 404,000 – had brought the provision up to the number required using the Education Department's formula of one school child for every six members of the by now increased population. By this time, London's 'visitors' – the agents who were charged with enumerating the children for the Statistical Committee – were estimating that an additional 78,000 places were needed.

There were constant arguments within the Board and between the Board and the Education Department about the number of school places which were needed. Some of the elements in the discussion have a familiar ring. It was not only the growth in population, nor yet the greater appetite for education, which had to be met. There was also internal migration: Southwark might have empty places and a declining population, while rural Catford and Lewisham had acute pressure of numbers.

Accusations of extravagance and over-provision were part of the stock-in-trade of the 'economists' on the Board, who had little difficulty in finding some statistical support for their opinions in view of the relatively crude measures which were employed. Yet the numbers of school places continued to rise (though more slowly) during the period between 1885 and 1894 when the Moderates were in control of the Board and the accent was on tighter financial control.

By the end of the period a new formula had been evolved. This assumed that school places would be required for all children aged 3 to 13 less 12½ per cent, plus the number of children over the age of 13 in the schools. The over-13s had begun to grow – in 1883 they numbered 16,644 (2·3 per cent of the 3–13 population). By 1898 the number had risen to 52,717, or 6·3 per cent, a growth which the Board attributed* to 'the general advance in public opinion in the appreciation of the value of education' and which they were convinced would continue to grow.

In the poorer districts, parents generally are still anxious to send their children to work as soon as they have reached the age of 13; but in other districts the better paid artisans and others who set a higher value on education for their children keep them at school as long as possible in larger numbers than hitherto.

The number of children in the Church and other voluntary schools fluctuated between 250,000 and 270,000 for most of the period. Only twelve years after the Board had come into existence, the number of children in its schools had caught up with the voluntary school population. By the end of the life of the School Board, London had 771,286 elementary school places: 554,198 of them in Board schools, 217,088 in voluntary schools.

Building schools

Even before the first survey of school numbers and accommodation had been completed in the spring of 1872, the first twenty new schools were sanctioned (in July 1871) – one in Chelsea, three in Finsbury, one in Greenwich, two in Hackney, one in Lambeth, four in Marylebone, three in Southwark, four in Tower Hamlets and one in Westminster. The Education Department acted with remarkable speed: the School Board asked for permission to go ahead on 6 July and received approval on 11 July. The first School Board school opened at the end of 1872 – two departments of the Berners Street School with room for 400 pupils. The following year twenty-eight more were provided to house another 22,000 children.

Seventy more followed in 1874. By 1876, the School Board had provided the 100,000 school places which had been called for in 1872. But each year

* London School Board Submission to Education Department, December 1898, quoted in the final report of the School Board.

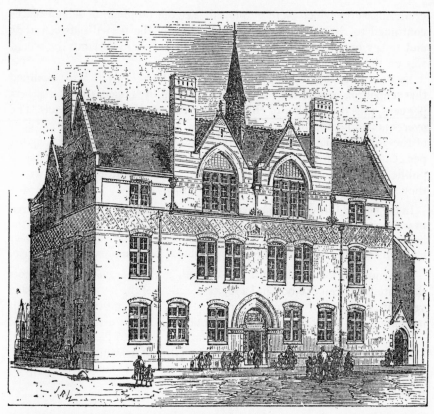

New Schools, Harper Street, New Kent Road, 1874.

the London 'elementary child population' was growing by 10,000, and the full extent of the need was becoming more apparent. By 1877, 140,000 permanent places had been provided; by 1880, 210,000; by 1890, 408,000; and by 1900, 531,500. Included in these totals were 56,663 places in 164 voluntary schools (mainly 'British') which were to be transferred to the Board mainly during the first few years. Few of the transferred schools could offer accommodation of a standard comparable with the schools which the Board built and 145 of them (with 53,082 places) were closed down as more up-to-date buildings came into service.

In a significant comment at the end of the section in the Board's final report there is a recognition that the Board schools were refusing the strict confines of social class which the educational and social theory of elementary education laid down. Quaintly, the Report noted that 'prior to the establishment of the School Board, one seventh of the population belonged to the class above that which uses Public Elementary schools; at the present time [1903] that class is only one tenth'.

Many of the schools built by the School Board still stand and, with more or less modification, remain in service. It was impossible to carry out a building programme of more than 600,000 school places in thirty years without learning a lot about school building and design. When the School Board came into existence, school design was simple in the extreme. The advice which the voluntary school authorities had received assumed that any barn or warehouse could provide the basic structure for a school. Many of the pre-1870 schools were housed in buildings which had been first put up for other purposes – houses, church and chapel buildings, workshops, the undercrofts of railway bridges. Often the buildings were as defective as the teaching.

As the old monitorial system was replaced by class instruction by teachers and pupil teachers, this had to be reflected in the buildings. By 1870, the conventional idea of a school as a single large room had been modified by the use of curtains or low partitions to divide up the space.

At the outset the School Board built on these lines, allowing eight square feet for each infant and nine square feet for the older children. Later, after prolonged arguments with the Education Department, this was increased to ten square feet and became a source of friction between the School Boards and the Churches, most of whose schools failed to come up to the ten-square-feet standard. (By the 1960s the space per child was averaging over seventy square feet per secondary child and forty square feet per primary child.)

The design had to correspond to the Board's expected staffing standards (1872):

The number of children to be taught by a certificated teacher, assisted by one pupil teacher, shall be 60. . . . For every additional 40 children there shall be an additional pupil teacher. And . . . for every additional 80 children, the increase of teaching power may be either one assistant certificated teacher, or two pupil teachers. As experience has shown that the separation or isolation of classes in separate rooms has an important bearing on results, the lessons contemplated under the six standards should, *as far as practicable*, be taught in separate classrooms.

The Board instructed its Works and General Purposes Sub-Committee to report on school design and equipment, and a resolution moved by

Mr 'Rob Roy' MacGregor listed qualities which a good school should possess. Nothing could show more clearly the heady atmosphere of the early days of the School Board. Schools should be made:

1. *Healthful*, by playgrounds and facilities for exercises and for bathing.
2. *Pleasant*, by children's games and music.
3. *Attractive*, by comfortable school furniture, simple tasteful decoration, wall-pictures, diagrams and flowers.
4. *Stimulative* to good conduct, attention, and progress by prizes.
5. *Instructive*, by illustrated lectures and by periodicals and publications suitable for children.
6. *Useful* to children of parents at work, by arrangements for dinner brought by the children, or provided by voluntary contributions.
7. *Influential* in after life, by a system of communication with scholars after they leave school and of certificates and rewards (from voluntary contributions) to those who retain situations and give satisfaction.

In reality the early Board Schools were extremely simple. Lord Lawrence opened the very first – Old Castle Street, Whitechapel – and described it as 'capitally well built, well lit, with five lofty rooms'.

The leaders in school architecture at this time were the Prussians who had pioneered the division of schools into classrooms of varying size and, in an elementary way, the relationship of the teaching spaces to the number of staff and the teaching methods. Controversy centred on the school hall. Was it still needed as a teaching space for several forms? Early design compromised by providing some classrooms but requiring some classes to be held in the hall. The first of a group of new experimental designs was the Johnson Street School at Stepney (later known as Ben Jonson) opened in 1873. The Education Department's grant regulations strictly limited the size. Corridors were provided but had to be used as cloakrooms which was 'inconvenient and dangerous'.* The classroom design became general and for a while no separate school hall was provided, though ingenious architects managed to provide a central corridor which could be used as a makeshift hall. In 1891 the grant regulations were altered and the central hall became a normal part of the design. Halls were added to many of the pre-existing schools.

From the first, the School Board had difficulty in acquiring sites. This forced the Board to think in terms of multi-storey buildings and large schools packed into small spaces. The original intention was to limit

* Final Report.

schools to 1,000 children. But soon the number was increased to 1,500 in three departments of 500 each, boys, girls and infants.

After relying on private architects for the first eighteen months, the Board appointed an official architect, E. R. Robson, who over the next thirty years became established as an international expert on school design. He was strongly critical of the early attempts which tried to cram too many children into too little space and personally presided over the steady progression from the early simple school rooms to the archetypal London three-deckers which had become a familiar part of the scene by the end of the century.

The simplicity of the early designs throws into relief the remarkable way in which standards rose and sophistication increased. Over the School Board period school building sites alone cost about £4 million. As the standards applied to new schools rose, the existing buildings had to be brought up to date by the addition of a school hall or the extension of class rooms.

Throughout the period many children were housed in 'iron schools' – prefabricated buildings which replaced the use of temporary hired premises and the least satisfactory of the transferred schools. Even at the end of the School Board's life there were still iron schools in action – in 1899, there were twenty-three such schools in sixty-two iron buildings and providing 8,000 places.

Later buildings incorporated three halls, one on each floor, for the boys, girls and infants. The architects began to be more conscious about lighting – mainly by gas and, as an expensive experiment, by electricity – and heating. Central heating and a crude form of air conditioning was installed experimentally at eight schools, starting with the 'Plenum' system at a Whitechapel school. The Final Report of the School Board commented acidly: 'as might have been expected in the first instance, the experiment was not a success'. One of the later schools to have a novel system was John Ruskin at Camberwell. The log books begin by referring repeatedly (and proudly) to the important visitors from far and wide who came to admire it. Later there are pained references to overheating and fumes which were liable to make the hall unusable. The Board's heating engineers were able to show that 'the air is changed much more frequently than in ordinary schools and is purer', but 'it cannot be disputed that the personal testimony of those frequenting the schools does not agree with the observations recorded by science'.

As a public authority building on a large scale, the School Board adopted a special clause in all building contracts for 1889 onwards, requiring any contractor carrying out work for the Board to promise to pay his workmen not less than the agreed minimum rate for each job. The conditions were later extended to other contractors supplying furniture, heating apparatus and other services.

In 1874 the Board set up its own store for the purchase of books, stationery and equipment, which in 1896 was transferred to a new building in Clerkenwell. Schools received requisition lists and could only choose from those books and other items which had been approved by the Board. From 1889 onwards light furniture was also bought centrally and provided for the schools from store.

Attendance

Counting the children and building schools for them was only one part of the task of setting up a London elementary school service. The parallel operation was to get the children into the schools.

The 1870 Act introduced compulsion but did so in the most tentative way. It was up to each School Board to decide whether to prepare bye-laws which, if approved by the Queen in Council, could compel parents to send their children to school. Sanctions behind these compulsory powers were the threat of a 5s. fine or, in certain circumstances, the removal of the child to an Industrial or truant school – early forerunners of Approved schools.

In spite of all the doubts and hesitations – the echoes of Brougham's thunder against compulsory education as a symbol of despotism – Matthew Arnold's twenty-year conviction that 'education will never, any more than vaccination, become general in this country until it is made compulsory' prevailed and the law was strengthened. In 1876 Sandon's Act imposed a duty on the parent to ensure his child received elementary education and required all School Boards to set up School Attendance Committees instead of leaving the decision to local judgement. Four years later, in 1880, it was formally enacted that all school attendance committees should introduce bye-laws and the familiar pattern had been followed whereby the practice of the more energetic authorities, of whom London was one, had become the standard to be applied elsewhere.

It was recognized from the outset that school attendance was as much a matter of social work as of legal enforcement. The London School Board was determined to be cautious. Enforcement, it was insisted, was 'to be

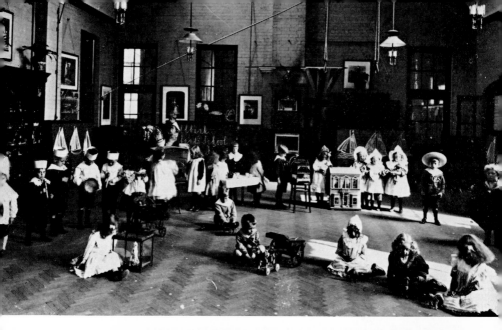

From the 1880s, schools were being encouraged to use kindergarten methods in the nursery classes and to allow these methods to spread upwards into the infants' school.
Top Children playing with toys in the babies' class at Millbank Infants' School, 1907. *Bottom* A game of skittles to introduce children to numbers at Southfields Infants' School, 1908.

The children's work is used to decorate the class room, but the large class still sits in ordered ranks. Flint Street, 1908.

Infant drama – also at Flint Street, 1908. Recitation: 'The sick dolly'.

At work in the school garden: Southfields Infants' School, 1906.

The class room out of doors at Wandle School, Earlsfield, 1911. The large playground is the scene of a dramatization of King Alfred burning the cakes.

The chemistry laboratory at Thomas Street School, 1908.

In the playground at Hague Street, Bethna
Green, a boys' practical geography class is
engaged in 'finding the true North'.

Children at Shrewsbury House open-air school studying pond life.

Dennis Butt.   Class 5

Nature Study

The History of the Frog

The home of the frog is in damp or swampy places. When it first comes out of its egg it is called a tadpole.

It is only head and tail, with two gills. When it is a few days old, there appear on each side of it, just near the tail, two little swellings, which burst after a time, and out come two little legs.

About a month after two more little swellings appear higher up, and then two more legs appear.

From a folio of work presented by
Halstow Road School, Greenwich, in 1907.

The regime at the Industrial schools –
forerunners of the Approved schools –
was tough and rigorous. It included basic
vocational instruction in various trades.
On discharge pupils were helped to find
employment or start life again in the
colonies or on the land.
Top A workshop scene at Feltham
Industrial School, 1908. *Bottom* Roll-call
for a party from St Nicholas School, *en
route* for Canada.

A Hebrew lesson in session at the Jews Free School, about 1906–8.

Domestic economy was taught at centres serving groups of schools where the girls attended one half-day a week. The aim was to teach children to be efficient housewives. 'All the work is based on scientific principles and in practice has to be done at the lowest possible cost and with the least possible waste.'

Instruction in laying a fire at Dulwich Hamlet, 1907.

Cleaning windows and scrubbing the steps at Surrey Lane, 1908.

SPECIAL SCHOOLS   In addition to general education (including Braille for the blind children and lip-reading for the deaf) the special schools aimed to equip handicapped children to be self-supporting with courses in rug-making, typewriting, music, etc.

Basket-making at Linden Lodge School for the Blind, 1908.

Open-air schools for delicate children – including those suffering from tuberculosis – put the emphasis on rest and fresh air.

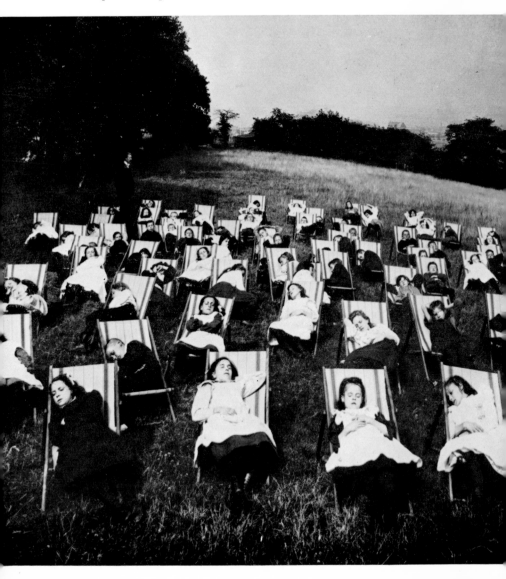

Growing interest in child health in the years before 1914 saw the beginnings of a school medical service.
Top Inspecting heads for ringworm and other parasites at Chaucer Street School, 1911. *Bottom* The school doctor's medical inspection, Holland Street, also 1911.

carried out especially at first with as much gentleness and consideration for the circumstances and feelings of the parents as is consistent with its effective operation'.

Local school attendance committees were set up on a divisional basis throughout the London area. Each division had a superintendent – at £200 a year – and a team of visitors who carried out the case work. Men visitors were paid £80 a year; women got £50. The work was hard and discouraging, particularly at the start when the appearance of 'the School Board man' (or woman) aroused abuse and vilification, not to mention missiles and threats of violence.

After the initial period when too few visitors wrestled with large numbers of children – by 1874 – visitors were appointed on the basis of one to every 3,000 children. Each had an area and a list of children to account for, visiting the homes of absentees and ferreting out the children who were not on the roll of any school.

Every spring they carried out their own census of children in all houses with a rateable value of £28 a year or less – another definition of the elementary school class. If it was not till the early 1890s that the numbers presented by the visitors had reached and began to exceed the rule-of-thumb projections based on the census figures, it seems likely that the correct explanation is the one accepted at the time – that, as methods of enforcing school attendance became more efficient, visitors succeeded in tracing and recording more of the children and the resistance of those who sought to hide children from official eyes became less.

Prosecution was only the last stage in a process. Before court proceedings were started, the divisional committees had to issue first an A notice, drawing the parent's attention to the bye-laws and inviting him to appear before the Committee to discuss his child's case. If this failed the B notice followed, threatening prosecution but again giving the parent the opportunity to explain the background. If the trouble was genuine and grinding poverty, the visitor could help to find a free school or the Board could waive the school fees. Charities could be approached for children who lacked school clothes or boots. Parents were advised and coaxed and generally helped to cooperate.

If, finally, a summons followed, this was often ineffective because the stipendiary magistrates, preoccupied with a long list of police-court business, were often impatient of school attendance cases. The London School Board repeatedly complained to the Home Office and the Lord Chancellor from 1873 onwards. By the 1890s attitudes had changed –

though there was continuing evidence of the uneven way in which courts handed out summary justice. At the end of the century school attendance was costing about £50,000 a year, employing 318 visitors and sixty-five clerical staff. In 1900 there were 28,836 summonses, of which 26,119 were successful.

School attendance was a matter of which teachers, and particularly head teachers, were made to feel acutely aware. There was resentment of the accusations made from time to time in School Board meetings, that poor attendance was the fault of the teachers and their failure to hold the attention and interest of their children. Friday afternoons and Monday mornings were times when attendance flagged. School log books show the ingenuity with which heads wooed the children with treats and outings, geared to the pattern of truancy. A magic lantern show or game of cricket was often as effective as a visit from the School Board man in roping the children in.

Bad attendance was linked with the whole question of child employment, vagrancy and the squalor in which children lived in the worst slums. Many of the children who were persistent truants worked long hours for minimal wages in one form of labour or another. A survey carried out by the London School Board in 1899 in 112 schools produced some disturbing figures about the amount of work children did out of school hours. Some 1,143 put in from 19 to 29 hours a week in employment, a further 729 worked 30–39 hours. And 285 worked for forty hours a week or more, over and above their normal school time. A measure of the pressure on the children can be gained from the paltry earnings they received. The largest group (1,056) were employed in shops and factories, working an average of thirty hours a week at 1½d. an hour. Some 719 averaged thirty hours a week delivering milk or selling newspapers at 1d. an hour; 309 did domestic work at ½d. an hour, while the remaining sixty-nine averaged twenty-nine hours a week at 1½d. an hour. Many of these jobs, like milk delivery or newspaper selling, got children out of bed early and kept them up late. Head teachers recorded their tendency to fall asleep and, often mercifully, recognized their handicaps.

Many hard-core truants lived rough. The riverside area, the railway termini, the purlieus of Drury Lane and Seven Dials, the streets and courts of Holborn and the Strand, the slums of the Borough, Whitechapel, Stepney and Bethnal Green, teemed with undernourished, frightened and brutalized children, many of them quite young. They slept under railway arches, on the steps of London Bridge, 'in empty boxes and boilers at

Bankside' and 'in empty packing cases down the Shades'. A favourite haunt for them was said to be George's Coffee House, otherwise known as the House of Lords in Upper Thames Street, where a room was specially set aside for them. In a famous passage one of the early school visitors described life in Boundary Street, Bethnal Green:

There were twenty-three public houses and beershops. Two general shops where spirits could be obtained at any time by those in the secret. Many of the public houses had a way right through so that persons could escape at the back and be easily lost in the streets behind. Examples of these were the 'Old Fountain' in High Street, Shoreditch; the 'Five Inkhorns', New Nicol Street; and the 'Admiral Vernon' in Old and New Nicol Streets. . . .

A number of the streets had many private houses through which persons could pass with little difficulty into other streets. The occupation of the women was chiefly matchbox making, and the manufacture of small articles for selling in the streets, and in these occupations the children had to bear a constant part.

The whole moral tone was inconceivably low. The people's lives consisted of constant deception and concealment. There was scarcely a family but appeared to have some reason for fearing the police, and a large proportion of the men were on 'ticket of leave'. . . .

Pickpockets, burglars, dog-stealers and pugilists here abounded. They might frequently be observed examining their tools on the window sills, and practising robbery from upper windows. Jim Smith, the pugilist, lived in Old Nicol Street, and attended Nicol Street Board School. Bill Goode, also – whose father was perhaps the most famous dog-stealer of his time – lived in New Turnville Street; Burdett, of Boundary Street, had 'done time' for horse stealing; his wife's father was concerned, with two others, in a burglary at Muswell Hill, when a young man was murdered, and they were arrested in the 'Barley Mow' in Boundary Street; James Baker, hanged for shooting a police inspector, after burglary, lived in the district. A murder was committed at 4 Old Nicol Street.

The children's lives were a constant round of sunless drudgery – they never played as children play, they never seemed even to think; they were prematurely old, and the victims of an awful cruelty. They worked at matchbox making many hours, and at other times assisted their parents in disposing of their wares in the streets. The mortality among the young children was appalling.

A child found begging or thieving, or brought up as 'beyond parental control', could be sent to a residential Industrial school. Some of these had been established during the previous twenty years under the Industrial Schools Act, 1866, and experimental legislation introduced in 1861 and 1862, and the Reformatory Act of 1854.

Others were established by the London and other School Boards. They came under the Home Office, not the Education Department, and were tough penal institutions. They were punitive and retributive in conception, and in a day when life outside these institutions was bleak and savage for the class of children who found their way inside, the regime had to be correspondingly severe if it was to be regarded as a deterrent. In some Industrial schools the prison atmosphere even included a preliminary spell of oakum picking and isolation in locked cells.

Part of the idea was to send children away from evil influences, and many London children found their way to Industrial schools in the country or in other towns. The tough regime included low standard education, some trade or craft instruction, and much physical education of the kind then in vogue. As the Home Office inspector put it: 'to keep a boys' school sweet and clean there is absolutely nothing so efficacious as a gymnasium'. By common consent, a good birch rod came a close second. Altogether the London School Board used some sixty-four voluntary Industrial schools – thirty-eight for boys and twenty-six for girls – and established nine of its own, including the two truant schools.

One of the London Industrial schools was the training ship *Shaftesbury*, taking in boys with no serious criminal record and, as well as keeping them under control, giving them a training to help them find a billet in the Royal Navy or the Merchant Service. As a means of preparing boys for a life at sea, it was not an immediate success. But gradually both services came to recognize the value of the training, both of skills and of character, which *Shaftesbury* offered. Figures for 1899 showed that twenty-five went to the Royal Navy, fifty-seven to the Merchant Navy, eighteen to the Army and sixty-three to other jobs ashore.

One of the preoccupations of the Industrial Schools Committee was to see that boys and girls who had passed through these schools were (as the saying went) properly 'disposed of'. Favoured forms of 'disposal' included, besides joining the Army, Navy or Merchant Marine, going on the land and emigration (provided there was nothing serious in the way of a criminal record). Later the Colonies became more fussy, but Canada continued to take a regular supply of London's Industrial school graduates.

By the end of the period, as well as the divisional visitors, each with his or her list, the School Board employed eleven experienced officers as unattached 'kid catchers', traversing London in search of children who could not explain their absence from school. Parks and open spaces were their happy hunting grounds. It is said that they found Punch and Judy shows good bait and were even in collusion with the showmen.

When a child was judged to be a persistent and incorrigible truant, he could be sent to a truant school. These, too, were cheerless, deterrent institutions intended to give youngsters a sharp jolt. According to one of the Board's inspectors, Dr P. B. Ballard, looking back, these seemed to him to be 'one dark spot on the Board's record'. The regimen was 'harsh and despotic', with 'discipline severe to the point of inhumanity' – a minimum of talking or conversation, little opportunity to play, no relaxation.

Discipline was strict. Older boys acted as monitors with the enthusiasm of reformed poachers. An eyewitness at Highbury Truant School described the 'almost uncanny' precision of the drill movements carried out by the boys.

For the greater part of the day they are under orders, performing every duty by word of command. Watch them, for example, coming to take their places for the afternoon meal. They march in in single file and sidle along to their places at the long tables with the short, rhythmic steps of soldiers 'closing up' on parade. . . . An officer plays a few chords on the harmonium, then raps sharply with a stick or mallet. Instantly all eyes are closed and the hands placed in an attitude of prayer; then grace is sung, not unpleasingly, though many of the voices are of coarse texture. When the verse is ended, there is not a movement till the rap is heard again; then the hands are brought down sharply and simultaneously to the sides and all stand at attention.

As residential institutions, Industrial schools were expensive – it cost about 10s. a week to keep a child at an Industrial school compared with 1s. 6d. or so a week at an ordinary elementary school. After many doubts and delays, the Board started its first day Industrial school – open 6 A.M. to 6 P.M. – in a disused elementary school building in Drury Lane in 1895. It was not intended for hard-core cases but for 'a class between the truant school and the industrial school class' – children had to have 'a fairly decent and respectable home, however poor'.

Many of the children [according to a contemporary account quoted by Spalding] are a rickity lot, of whom any savage nation would be ashamed, and whom an ancient Greek would probably have weeded out by some summary process of selection. They are pale, flaccid, and headachy, symptoms accompanied by sores at the angles of the mouth and nose, and at the junction of the ears with the head. Their food is well prepared but . . . they are dainty, wanting in appetite and sometimes even averse to food. Of the 116 children admitted within the year, 47 were below the average height, 86 were below the average weight, 79 were below the average chest measurements. Only a minority, in fact, were really healthy or perfectly formed children.

The success of the day Industrial schools was immediate and impressive when it was discovered that deprived children respond to kindness and three square meals a day better than they do to a regime of penal toughness. A second school of a similar type was opened at Brunswick Road, Poplar, in 1901.

The outcome of all the effort – organization, visitation, social work, encouragement, prosecution, punishment – can be measured in two ways. The first is a measure of the success of the visitors in their task of identifying and enumerating the children and getting them on to school rolls. The second is the rising average percentage attendance of those on school rolls.

London's child population was rising throughout the School Board's life – from an estimated 570,000 in 1871 to over 880,000 by the early years of the new century. Average daily attendance at public elementary schools, however, rose from 173,000 to about 650,000, and the average percentage attendance of those on the rolls from about seventy per cent at the beginning of the period to eighty-one per cent by the end. (Attendance at the Board's schools – eighty-four per cent – was rather higher than at the voluntary schools.)

The Board refused to regard this as satisfactory. In 1901 the school attendance service was strengthened and the case-load for each visitor reduced from 3,000 to 2,800 so that a special drive could be made on children who were only averaging eight sessions out of ten each week. In reality, however, the figure was no mean achievement in view of the fact that compulsion did not apply to the under-5s (of whom there were no fewer than 76,000 on roll) or to those aged 10 or over who had passed standard five or took advantage of the various half-time exemptions for those 'beneficially and necessarily' in employment.

The profile of the elementary school population was such that, even at the end of the period, there were as many pupils aged 6 and under, as 11 and over.

3 A curriculum for the Board schools

Even before the Board had any schools to administer, a sub-committee was set up to draw up a scheme of education – a curriculum, in fact. The man chosen to preside over this was the academic doyen of the first Board, Professor T. H. Huxley. The sub-committee reported in four months – after sixteen meetings and taking evidence from thirteen practising teachers – and, with minor amendments, its proposals, in the following terms, were accepted by the Board as a whole in the summer of 1871:

In Infants' schools instruction shall be given in the following subjects:
(a) The Bible and the Principles of Religion and Morality. . . .
(b) Reading, Writing and Arithmetic.
(c) Object lessons of a simple character, with some such exercise of the hands and eyes as is given in the Kindergarten System.
(d) Music and Drill.

In Junior and Senior Schools certain kinds of instruction shall form the essential part of the teaching of every school; but others may, or may not, be added to them at the discretion of the Managers of individual schools, or by the special direction of the Board. The instruction in the discretionary subjects shall not interfere with the efficiency of the teaching of the essential subjects.

The following subjects shall be essential:
(a) The Bible and the Principles of Religion and Morality. . . .
(b) Reading, Writing and Arithmetic; English Grammar and Composition and the principles of Bookkeeping in the Senior schools; with Mensuration in Senior Boys' schools.
(c) Systematized Object Lessons, embracing in the six school years a course of elementary instruction in Physical Science and serving as an introduction to the science examinations which are conducted by the Science and Art Department.
(d) The History of England.
(e) Elementary Geography.

HOUSEWIFERY.

(I) GUIDING PRINCIPLES TO ENSURE HEALTH AND HAPPINESS.

(a) In selecting a house see that it is thoroughly drained, well-lighted, and capable of thorough ventilation.

(b) Endeavour to obtain a knowledge of the chief elements of food, their uses, and the best methods of cooking.

(c) Learn the best methods of keeping your home thoroughly clean and wholesome.

(d) Study how to PREVENT disease as well as how to restore to health those who are sick.

(e) Provide recreations and amusements in the home so that the members of the family may be made happy and kept from seeking their pleasures in questionable places.

(f) Be careful and thrifty so that you may be independent in your old age.

(2) COST OF FURNISHING A WORKING MAN'S HOME.

SITTING-ROOM—	£	s.	d.
Four chairs -	0	16	0
Two easy chairs	1	5	0
Strong deal table	1	2	6
Fender - -	0	13	9
Fire irons - -	0	9	6
Curtains - -	0	5	6
Table Cover -	0	8	6
Screen - -	0	9	0
Small table -	0	7	6
Lamp (safety) -	0	16	0
Pictures and ornaments - -	1	0	0
Rug - - -	0	12	9
Linoleum (good) -	1	10	0
BED-ROOM—			
Bed (complete) -	3	10	0
Two chairs -	0	6	0
Washstand -	0	10	6
Deal toilet table -	0	7	6

	£	s.	d.
Cover for same -	0	3	0
Curtains - -	0	2	6
Straw-matting -	1	0	0
Chamber ware -	0	3	11
Blankets, sheets, counterpane -	1	15	0
Fender - -	0	6	0
Towel horse -	0	3	6
Bath - - -	0	2	3
Folding bed (complete) - -	4	12	0
KITCHEN—			
Earthenware and cutlery - -	2	10	0
Washing & cleaning utensils -	4	10	0
	£29	18	2

An L.S.B. notice for display in housecraft centres, issued in 1891.

(f) Elementary Social Economy.
(g) Elementary Drawing.
(h) Music and Drill.
(i) (In Girls' schools) Plain needlework and cutting out.
  The following subjects shall be discretionary:
(a) Domestic Economy.
(b) Algebra.
(c) Geometry.
  Subject to the approbation of the Board, any extra subjects recognised by the new Code, 1871, shall be considered to be discretionary subjects.

The Huxley Committee also laid down principles for school organization. There were to be separate departments for infants, juniors and seniors. Each Board school under one body of managers would contain an infants' school, a junior school, a senior boys' school and a senior girls' school. Infants' schools were to be mixed; senior schools were to be single sex; while for junior schools there was to be no fixed rule.

From the first, large schools were envisaged. 'Junior and Senior schools of 500 upwards can be worked with much greater economy and efficiency than small schools'. Infants' departments were to be pegged at 250–300.

Staffing requirements were generous by the standards of the time – 'the minimum number of teachers required for a junior or senior school of 500 should be 16 – a head, four certificated assistants and eleven pupil teachers, and thereafter the staff should rise by one assistant and three pupil teachers for every 120 additional pupils. Women teachers were held to be suitable only for teaching infants and girls. Each day was to include five hours of instruction and the schools were to work a five-day week in term-time.

The sub-committee also defined the Board's policy on corporal punishment. This was permitted (though its 'frequent use . . . is a mark of incompetency on the part of the teacher') by the head in person. It was absolutely prohibited to pupil teachers and a resolution three years later applied this ban to all other assistant teachers. In 1888 the ban was relaxed and assistants were allowed to use the cane if given authority in writing by the head. All punishments had to be recorded.

This change followed a series of incidents which brought to a head a running battle which the teachers and their union, the Metropolitan Board Teachers' Association, had waged with the Board. The teachers wanted the same right to chastize children as the common law allowed

them when acting *in loco parentis*. The Board was all along more inclined
to restrict corporal punishment.

The use of the cane was an issue on which leading figures – notably
some of the formidable women members – campaigned. None was more
vehement than Miss Helen Taylor, John Stuart Mill's stepdaughter, who
represented Southwark from 1876 to 1885. Another powerful, though more
silent, opponent was Miss Rosamond Davenport Hill, once publicly
described as 'the adorable spinster'. She was an expert on Industrial
schools and knew how savage physical punishments could become commonplace in a bad school.

But the task of teachers in maintaining discipline was often difficult in
the slum areas where compulsory attendance was resented and assaults on
teachers by irate and muscular parents were commonplace.* An attempt by
two members, the Rev. Mark Wilks and Miss Davenport Hill, to have the
head of Mansford Street School, Bethnal Green, sacked for allowing his
assistants to inflict corporal punishment was defeated (a fine and reprimand
was imposed instead) and a few months later, after a teacher at Dulwich
Hamlet School had been the victim of blackmail by a parent after striking a
child, the rule was relaxed.

There were three items in the curriculum put in by the School Board
before the sub-committee started work – religious instruction, music and
physical training or drill. The first caused lengthy controversy in London
as elsewhere. The law was strictly negative. It laid down that denomina-
tional doctrines must not be taught; that instruction, if given at all, must
only be in the first or last period of the day; that no child should be
required to attend a Church or Sunday School as a condition of enrolment;
and that parents should have the right to withdraw their children if they
wished to do so.

Four members voted against religious instruction – among them the
Rev. William Rogers, rector of St Botolph's, Bishopsgate, an undogmatic
Anglican. The rest were agreed that the Bible should be taught but divided
on how much interpretation should be given. Mr. W. H. Smith, M.P.,
resolved the argument with a carefully worded formula: 'that in the
schools provided by the Board the Bible shall be read, and then shall be
given such explanations and such instruction therefrom in the principles
of morality and religion as are suited to the capacities of the children'.

* Some like James Runciman, brother of the ship-owner, returned like with like. An
entry in his Deptford School log book is said to have run: 'Father of boy – came to school
today and was very disorderly; I carried him out and chastized him.'

The Huxley curriculum represented another example of the idealism of the first Board. It looked beyond the immediate situation to an educational scene which did not exist, nor could exist for a generation. It was attacked as over-ambitious by rate-payer associations and the vestries who had the task of raising the education rate. It was, moreover, palpably impossible to achieve in the first Board schools and in the transferred and temporary schools of the early 1870s. By 1873, in the final report of the first Board, the Clerk, Mr G. H. Croad, stated that the scheme had been carried out 'as far as practicable with the very raw material to be found for the most part in Board schools. It could not,' he went on, 'of course be regarded otherwise than as an ideal; to which, however, the Board hope that their schools will approximate more and more with each succeeding year.'

One of those who attacked the Board was Matthew Arnold. In his report on schools in Westminster in 1878 he contrasted London's costs with those of schools elsewhere in England – London's costs per pupil were 53s. 5d. a year, compared with a national average of 35s. 3d.

. . . I am quite sure [he wrote], that their conception of what is requisite in the way of accommodation, studies, salaries, administration, is pitched too high. Both in London and elsewhere, school boards are apt to conceive what is requisite in these respects rather as benevolent, intelligent, and scientific educationalists in utopia than as practical school managers. . . . It is evident that secondary and superior education must come to be on an insupportable scale of expense, if the expense of even elementary institutions is to be 55s. 11d. a year for every scholar. . . . I am desirous of seeing secondary education instruction made a public service. But the prodigality of our present outlay on elementary tuition interposes an obstacle. . . .

Arnold's strictures are understandable in the light of his anxiety to persuade the Education Department to set the secondary education system in order, but the pace-setting quality of the London School Board's efforts was vindication enough. It may be that the method by which London precepted on the vestries for funds had something to do with it but more than anything else there was the determination that, in laying the foundations of a public system of education, the School Board should aim high, not low. In time there would be no lack of critics who saw their task as that of guardians of the rate-payers' money.

Huxley's ambitious conception of elementary education had to be contrasted with that of the Education Department's Codes, which also exerted a direct influence on the schools and the teachers. The Codes were the basis on which Government grants – amounting at first to around forty per cent of what it cost to educate a child at a London Board school – were paid. Since the Revised Code of 1862 had introduced Sir Robert Lowe's principle of payment by results, the grants were pinned to the specific performance of individual children in the six standard examinations conducted by Her Majesty's inspectors. This continued with modifications at intervals till 1890 – a turning point in the history of the Board – when the hated payment by results came to an end and grants were based on attendance.

The London School Board boldly refused to base the curriculum on the limited range of activities on which grant was paid. Successive Codes expanded the list of optional or class subjects on which, in addition to the three Rs and needlework, grant was payable, but schools were not allowed to present any child for examination in more than two or three class subjects.

From the first, Huxley's view of elementary education included the need to set up a ladder leading on to secondary schooling. In a note he appended to the curriculum report, it was pointed out that:

The Elementary Education Act does not confer upon a School Board the power of providing secondary schools, and it is silent as to the mode by which a connection may be established between the elementary and secondary schools of the country. But it is of such importance to the efficacy of popular education that means should be provided by which scholars of more than average merit should be enabled to pass from elementary into secondary schools, that we feel it our duty to offer some suggestions upon the subject.

The practical difficulty in the way of the passage of boys and girls from an elementary into a secondary school is the cost of their maintenance, and the best way of meeting that difficulty appears to be to establish exhibitions equivalent to the earnings of boys and girls from 13 to 16 years of age tenable for the periods during which they remain under instruction in the secondary schools. The funds out of which such exhibitions may be created already exist, and the machinery for distributing them has been provided by the Legislature in the Endowed Schools Act.

How the links were formed belongs largely to another chapter, but by the 1890s school log books began to record the scholarships and Honour boards displayed the names of those – several hundred each year – who won places at Christ's Hospital and at London endowed grammar schools. The chain was strengthened when the Technical Education Board was set up by the London County Council in 1891, and decided that a major part of its work would be to provide scholarships and exhibitions to secondary schools.

For a long time, however, the London curriculum, though it offered opportunity and relative freedom for some, was mocked by the state of the schools and the pressures of the grant system. The first ten years were grey and discouraging; academic achievement was low; it was enough to concentrate on getting children into school and on taming and socializing those older children who had come reluctantly without the advantages of an infant's schooling. It took ten years to get the school-going habit established and during this time the high aims of the Huxley curriculum were more honoured in the breach than in the observance.

In 1883 the Codes were modified in a manner which stepped up still further the pressure on the teachers. Instead of a flat rate of payment for each successful pupil in the H.M.I.'s examination, the value of the grant was to be dependent on the average level of success attained by each class as a whole.

The idea was plain enough – a financial instrument to raise the standard of class teaching as a whole. The result was to accentuate pressure on the schools in their attempts to carry out the ambitious curriculum devised by the Board, while at the same time responding to the narrow, yet tough demands of the Code.

By the year 1885 public anxiety about educational standards and the effect of the examination system had built up into what became known as the 'overpressure' controversy. It was aided by an alarmist report by a medical officer, Dr Crichton Browne, that the expansion of public education was driving children into mental and physical breakdowns.

The fires of controversy were stoked by the School Board election of 1885 when the Moderates broke the Progressives' hold on the London School Board and the redoubtable Rev. J. R. Diggle succeeded Mr E. N. Buxton as chairman.

What the overpressure controversy did was to bring into a single focus a variety of different defects in the system. It linked the social and pedagogic deficiencies – the ill-effects caused by mechanical teaching and the physical consequences of inadequate diet and poor housing. It stepped up the demand for a curriculum with more limited aims and in particular more attention to practical and vocational studies.

A sub-committee was set up in 1887 with Mr William Bousfield, a Chelsea member, as chairman, to consider 'Subjects and Modes of Instruction'. The terms of reference indicated the thinking behind this revision of the Huxley programme. The committee was 'to consider the present subjects and modes of instruction . . . and report whether such changes can be made as shall secure that children leaving school shall be more fitted than they now are to perform the duties and work of life before them'.

The new curriculum proposals were contained in twenty-nine recommendations adopted by the Board in 1888. The following are a selection:

1. That the methods of Kindergarten teaching in Infants' schools be developed for senior scholars throughout the Standards in schools, so as to supply a graduated course of Manual Training in connection with Science teaching and Object lessons. . . .

3. That the Board encourage Modelling in Clay in all departments of schools, both in connection with Drawing as a training of the artistic faculties, and for the illustration of the teaching of Geography and other subjects. . . .

5. That, as soon as the Board are permitted by law to give special instruction in manual work, such instruction shall be given to boys in and above the Fourth Standard. . . .

6. That classes for instruction in Slöjd be established in three selected schools approved by the School Management Committee [Slöjd was a novel Swedish form of handicraft teaching]. . . .

11. That instruction in Practical Geometry be included in the teaching of Drawing, and that Mechanical Drawing to scale with actual measurements be encouraged in all Boys' departments.

12. That instruction in Drawing be given in all Girls' departments, though it be not taken as a subject of examination.

13. That instruction in Cookery be given only to Girls over 11 years of age without regard to Standard, and that the necessary additional Cookery Centres be provided.

14. That the time now given for Dictation be reduced in all Standards, and that in substitution for the part omitted in the lower Standards the reproduction by children in their own words of passages read out to them, and in Standard IV and upwards original composition be taken.

15. That the teaching of Reading should be specially directed to give children an interest in books, and to encourage them to read for their own pleasure, and that Reading books should be for imparting a knowledge of Geography, History, Social Economy, and facts of common life to all children who may not be able to take such subjects for examination.

16. That, in order to allow time for experimental teaching and manual work, the time now given to Spelling, Parsing and Grammar generally be reduced.

17. That the Board authorise the appointment of an Organiser of Teaching, whose duties shall be to assist and advise teachers in the instruction of

manual work, and in an improved method of instruction by the development of Kindergarten training.

18. That the Board authorise the appointment of an Officer, whose duties shall be to give instruction in, and to organise, the methods of teaching Mechanical and Geometrical Drawing. . . .

21. That teachers be informed that the Board do not pay so much attention to the percentage of passes obtained at the Government Inspection as to the general tone and character of the school work. . . .

24. That Advanced Evening Classes be established at the various Pupil Teachers' Schools, for instruction in Science and Drawing, Commercial Subjects, and Modern Languages.

25. That the playgrounds attached to schools be used for the formation of clubs for hardy sports, gymnastic exercises and drill, and that the school organisations be used for the establishment of field clubs and swimming classes.

26. That the Chairman of the Board be asked to convene a meeting of local Managers and others to consider the question of organised Physical Education out of school hours, and to request personal help in the work. . . .

While the impetus was towards more practical, down-to-earth schooling, it is interesting to note that with this went a desire to see the kindergarten method penetrate upwards into the junior schools. Already the foundation of the modern primary school was being prepared, and action on recommendation number 17 meant that the Board had an organizer to attend to this. At the turn of the century, Miss Philips, Superintendent of Method for infants' schools, was able to write of the 'many influences which are gradually widening and liberalising elementary education' and leading to 'a more human conception of the infants school in the educational scheme'. Her tone is uncannily like that of the Hadow report of 1931 or the Plowden report of 1967:

A good result will not be produced in a later stage if the present stage be not lived through fully, freely and thoroughly; and the children developed freely and happily in mind and body . . . the infants' department is intended to give that training and instruction which the baby children, in other circumstances, would receive from the care of an intelligent, cultivated, educated mother, who could give a very large part of her time to her children. The little ones must live through the stage of early childhood in an atmosphere of affection, of cheerfulness, of reasonable freedom, and of constant joyous activity.

Miss Philips goes on to describe the kinds of activity she has in mind, including object lessons, singing, nature study, drawing, painting and modelling in clay and story-telling with an emphasis on language. Games and rhythmic movement are included. The infants' schools had presided over a revolution in methods of teaching reading – an incomplete revolution no doubt, but again, something with a very modern ring to it: 'each teacher makes for herself some bright interesting combination of "Look and Say" and Phonic method'.*

It was not till the Education Department's Code was modified in 1890 that manual training could legally be provided in the schools at public expense. London had started to offer woodwork for senior pupils in 1885 when the school keeper at the Beethoven Street School, Paddington (who happened to be a carpenter) turned his hand to it in a shed erected on the playground. The local government auditor disallowed the cost and, to keep it going, London had to raise money from the City Guilds.

Eventually the Education Department relented after the Liverpool School Board had obtained Counsel's opinion that manual instruction given by teachers on the school timetable could lawfully be provided out of school funds.

At first the woodwork instruction was strictly disciplinary – the making of mortise joints and similar craft exercises. Later the approach was liberalized and boys were allowed to make a start on the proverbial pipe-racks and egg trays.

During the 1880s the teaching of science in London schools was also overhauled, under the leadership of Dr J. H. Gladstone, F.R.S. – a member of the Board from 1870 to 1892, and father-in-law of Ramsay MacDonald. Dr Gladstone persuaded the London Board to adopt experimental methods of science teaching.

The episode is of considerable interest in the context of curriculum reform then and now, because it illustrated one of the practical lessons of educational innovation – that, to change the method, new teaching materials are required as well as new pedagogic insights. Dr Gladstone provided the new materials. He designed an inexpensive box of simple science apparatus 'for illustrating experimentally the elementary principles of chemistry and physics'. By 1887 four demonstrators had been recruited to introduce these new methods into schools.

---

* Miss Nellie Dale's system developed in the 1890s was the subject of courses and demonstrations for London infants' schools. It was a phonic method which was already beginning to use different colours to represent particular sounds on the blackboard, and in printed materials.

In 1891 the four science demonstrators started classes for teachers in different parts of London, and later this programme of in-service training was expanded by the School Management Committee. At the turn of the century, Dr Gladstone's pioneering attempts to encourage experimental methods of science teaching were reinforced by the widespread adoption of Professor Armstrong's 'heuristic' educational principles which added a respectable Greek name to the new approach.

Higher grade schools

Rising levels of achievement made it necessary to think beyond the seven standards into which elementary education had been divided, originally for the purposes of examination and the payment of grants. The child of 7 who moved into a junior school began in standard I, moving up (theoretically) each year on passing the H.M.I.'s examination. Originally there had been six standards. A seventh was instituted in 1882 for those who stayed longer or, as was quite possible, passed through the standards at a better than average speed. The trouble was that many pupils left at the earliest possible opportunity, from standard IV, V or below. Teaching groups in the upper standards were often too small to warrant a separate teacher.

In its classic simplicity the development of the higher grade school illustrates a sequence of recurring ideas in educational administration. The answer to small and inefficient teaching groups was to concentrate resources in a limited number of schools. In 1887 the Board resolved that only one school in every group of schools should provide instruction in the higher grades – that is standards V, VI and VII. These would become the higher grade or central schools. When these ideas were submitted to the Education Department their Lordships 'highly approved' the principle.

There were local criticisms, particularly at first. The scheme had its limitations. It was up to parents to transfer their children to the higher grade schools; the Board refused to put pressure on them. Heads of schools which had not been selected resented the attempt to deprive them of their cream, their social and sporting élite. But while some of the central schools made slow progress, others became so popular that parents contended to get their children in. This had the effect of making some of them more or less selective. Parents who wanted to be sure of a place at the favoured school competed to get their infants on the school roll, ignoring travelling difficulties.

But, all the same, the higher grade schools prospered, developing more work including science, modern languages and technical drawing, beyond standard VII, leading to the Oxford and Cambridge local examinations (which were accepted as preliminary qualifications for pupil teachers) and the examination of the London Chamber of Commerce. All the usual wiles were exerted to encourage more to persevere by awarding special Honours and Merit Certificates to successful pupils.

Whereas in 1886 there were some 48,605 boys and girls in standard V and above, by 1903 the number had risen to 105,022. Over the same period, the total number of London Board school children had risen from 375,000 to 544,000. Thus the higher grade work had expanded by 117 per cent while the total school population had only increased by about forty-five per cent. By the end of the century London had seventy-nine higher grade schools, four of which were recognized as 'schools of science' and received grants from the Science and Art Department for what was clearly secondary work.

At this point the political argument about publicly provided secondary education, and which were the most appropriate public authorities to administer it, overtook the whole hopeful development. London had hoped to be allowed to go on developing the higher grade schools as the natural efflorescence of the whole elementary school enterprise. When the newly created Board of Education issued a Minute in 1900 which offered special grants for higher grade schools and laid down new guide lines for them, the School Board submitted their seventy-nine candidates for the higher grade school list with genuine if misplaced optimism.

Instead of regarding the higher grade schools as an efficient method of organizing the upper sections of a normal elementary education, the new policy was to make the schools selective with a competitive examination at 11 and a firm leaving age of 15 at the end of a heavily science-orientated four-year course. The London School Board deplored this, but its own future was by now increasingly uncertain and it could do nothing but acquiesce. Only seven of London's seventy-nine higher grade schools were accepted.

The School Board era came to a close with the elementary school curriculum in retreat and a new and artificial rigidity introduced at just that point when it appeared the elementary school might have been about to develop extended education on an open-ended basis. Instead of establishing the circumstances in which those who wished might stay, on the principle of the emergence and later differentiation of talents, the rigid separation of elementary and secondary education was insisted upon, and with it the principle of selection by elimination. It need not have been so. But to have developed otherwise it would have been necessary to escape from the class-based conceptions of elementary and of secondary education. Secondary education remained a normal progression for the middle-class children – the principle of emergence – but for the elementary school classes secondary education represented a distinct and positive social movement – a transition only to be made by those able to prove by some early achievement that they were specially marked out from their fellows by 'a capacity to benefit' from secondary education. This selective principle was to dominate the development of secondary education over the next half-century.

4 *Sidelights*

An early move which helped to shape the style of London's school administration was the decision to administer the schools through bodies of managers. This was eminently sensible in view of the size of London, but not legally necessary. Each body of managers contained a member of the School Board and other local notabilities recommended by the member or by others. In transferred schools, the outgoing body of managers were invited to supply half the number. From 1873 onwards, the Board insisted that every body of managers must include a woman. At the centre was the School Management Committee of the Board.

The managers' duties were not unimportant. They selected and appointed heads of staff. (In 1889 the shortlisting of heads was taken over by the School Management Committee.) They investigated complaints against the staff which were many but in most cases trivial and frivolous. They had to appoint a health sub-committee, as part of the compaign against 'overpressure', to look after the welfare of the 'dull and delicate'. Each year they had to report on the health of the children, the curriculum, the state and use of libraries, the 'extra-scholastic' efforts of the school, the incidence of poverty and destitution and any special plans for interesting parents in the work of the schools. All in all, some 3,000 managers were appointed.*

By the turn of the century the Board schools in their massive three-decker buildings had established solid traditions and regular habits. One of the officers of the Board, S. E. Bray, contributed an idealized description of a day at such a school to Spalding's account of the work of the London School Board. The date is 1900. It is nine o'clock in the school playground:

---

* In 1889 it was resolved that 'as far as possible' every group of managers should include two parents or ex-parents of elementary school children. This came to little as the working men the Board was seeking had not the leisure time to perform the duties of managers, which included visits to the schools during the day.

The head master may blow his whistle at any moment as the signal for the various classes to fall into their allotted places, and the assistant teachers will suddenly appear as though they had sprung out of the ground. The whistle is blown. . . . The classes fall in two deep, with an assistant master in charge of each; they go through one or two simple evolutions in military drill, and then march through the playground in double file, ascend the staircase, and enter their respective class rooms. . . .

On the stroke of nine the class room doors are closed and the first act of registration is performed. . . . This accomplished, the Lord's Prayer is repeated, a few other preliminaries to the morning's work done, and the late-comers are admitted. The lesson in Scripture then begins. . . .

At 9.45 . . . the second act of registration begins by placing against each late-comer's name a mark or stroke in black ink. . . . The register being closed, the secular work of the school commences. . . . On consulting the time-table, hung in the hall or some other conspicuous position . . . which must be submitted to, and approved by, H.M. Inspector . . . one finds that arithmetic is being taught in one class, English grammar in another, geography in a third, elementary science in a fourth, and so on. These various lessons last for three quarters of an hour, which brings the time to 10.30 A.M. Work is then stopped and the whole school is marched into the playground, class by class, for ten minutes' recreation. On returning to their places in the usual order, each class receives instruction in another subject till 11.20, when another subject supplants the previous one till the clock announces mid-day. The school is then dismissed in the same orderly fashion as it entered the building. . . .

In the afternoon,

. . . the bell again rings out, the master's whistle is blown, and assembly takes place in the same way as in the morning. . . . The afternoon's work is much the same as the morning's; divided into three secular lessons of about forty minutes' duration, with a recreation interval coming between; except that, as a rule, the more difficult subjects, such as arithmetic and grammar, are taken in the morning, and the easier ones in the afternoon, as, for example, drawing, writing, composition, and singing. The boys and girls of the senior departments are dismissed at 4.30 P.M., and the infants half an hour earlier.

Although there is no rule forbidding home lessons, yet these are rarely given unless it be to scholars in the higher classes, and even then there are no sanctions by which they may be enforced. The Board, indeed, distinctly forbids punishment of any kind for failure to perform home tasks that may be imposed by the teachers. In schools, however, situated in the best districts, home lessons are generally well done, without causing those manifest inconveniences to the family which must arise when home accommodation is more limited.

As the morning's work is much like the afternoon's, so is one day very much the same as another in a week's school life, although the lessons rarely follow exactly the same order, and certain subjects are only taught once or twice from Monday morning to Friday afternoon. But those subjects that are rudimentary, as reading, writing, and arithmetic, recur, of course, with persistent regularity. Friday afternoon is made, in the bulk of the schools, the most attractive session of the week, because the attendance on that occasion shows a decided tendency to fall off. Teachers, therefore, in order to check this tendency, often read and expound to their classes some pretty stories culled from the works of distinguished writers, or show them some of the minute wonders revealed by the microscope, or take them on an imaginary journey through city, field and forest, as illustrated by the optical lantern, or tear a page from history and give it the touch of life by the same means. . . .

It may be said generally of the teaching, that though theory does, and must always play an important part, yet practical methods nearly everywhere prevail, and realities are introduced whenever it is possible. Any object that is fairly accessible and portable is obtained by the really keen teacher. Teaching by practical illustration is encouraged by the Board.

The school is at various times suddenly and unexpectedly called upon to go through its fire drill. . . .

The Log Book, kept by the head master, is a record of all important school events. In it may be read such entries as the following, under various dates:

1. Standard VI visited the South Kensington Museum in the afternoon.
2. Standard V had a field excursion to study botany.
3. All schools closed to-day by order, on account of the Annual Drill Display held at the Albert Hall.
4. T. Smith, H. Jones, and J. Brown each obtained the Junior County Scholarship, valued at £10 a year for two years.
5. In accordance with the Board's order to test the eyes of the children annually, in the month of July, the recognised tests were put into operation, and the children classified accordingly.

Swimming has not been mentioned as part of the school curriculum. This, however, is recognised in the summer months, both by the Education Department and the Board. As only one bath belongs to the Board, municipal and private baths have to be used. About 12,000 children belonging to the Board's day schools annually learn to swim; that is, roughly, one-third of those actually under instruction in that subject.

The girls' department is usually, as regards structure, a reproduction of the boys'. The rudimentary and class subjects are also much the same in both places. The girls, however, take up other work specially suitable to their sex, such as needlework, domestic economy, cookery, and laundry.

From this department one descends another flight of steps to the infants', where the two sexes work together. It is a pretty sight to see them go through their musical drill, and to observe how thoroughly they enjoy it. Many visitors remark on the deliciously soft voices among the older children and praise their singing, which for time and sweetness of tone cannot be surpassed by the boys and girls in the senior departments. Distributed over the department are to be found, in addition to pictures, excellent models of animals and sometimes globes of goldfish supplied by the teachers themselves. . . .

The impression, even allowing for Mr Bray's mode of expression, is of formal efficiency. There was the occasional maypole, the formal treat on great occasions; there was the 'massed drill in boots and heavy clothing' and the 'wrist and arm drill'.

With the variety of social circumstance which London comprised, any single picture must be grossly misleading, as a glance at a few of the log books demonstrates. John Ruskin School, Camberwell, at the turn of the century, is in a good neighbourhood. Its first scholars have begun to win scholarships – and their names to go up on the Honour Board – that essential piece of equipment in a progressive Board school. ('June 6th, 1902, Leonard Teakle, the first boy to win a scholarship from this school, left for the Blue Coat School.')

The log book reports the school's At Homes – the ambitious open days which would bring 200 parents into the buildings to admire work. It shows a confident staff planning school visits ('Mr Bright took 13 of his standard II boys to Greenwich going and returning by boat'), the rewards for good attendance by standard V and VI ('a lesson in cricket at 4 P.M.'), setting up a combined school choir, choosing school colours, adopting a school motto. . . .

Over at Smallwood Road, Tooting, however, life was more rugged. The school buildings are new but the surrounding streets are a shambles. 'The school is steadily increasing, and if the neighbouring roads were mended, the percentage of attendance would probably be considerably higher' reads a log book entry in 1895. 'Very heavy rain, consequently attendance poor. The Smallwood Road has not been repaired and is still covered with stagnant water. . . .' Other entries are a reminder of the prevalence – and seriousness – of childish illnesses – the outbreaks of measles and scarlet fever, the dreaded diphtheria and the fair expectation in a school of any size of a number of deaths each year.

Red letter days

There are the great occasions – Queen Victoria's eightieth birthday is good for a holiday; so is her funeral. King Edward's Coronation is marked by a whole week's holiday. There is the period's easy patriotism and unthinking national pride – Empire Day becomes a regular school fixture – 'the whole school assembled in the hall for prayers . . . the headmistress talked to the children about the Empire, size, parts, people, how brought together, description of the Union Jack, and what the children can do towards making the Empire good and great'.

Queen Victoria's Silver Jubilee in 1887 produced a magnificent celebration for London school children in Hyde Park, attended by 30,000 children chosen by ballot (weighted in favour of those with good attendance records). The Queen drove round in a carriage. The Rev. J. R. Diggle, then Chairman of the Board, was at the top of his form, handing out presents to the children from the specially purchased stock of 72,000 toys, 42,000 mugs, 30,000 medals, 1,000 Jubilee skipping ropes.

For entertainment there was Herr Winkelmeier, the Austrian giant reputed to be 8 feet 9 inches tall, and 1,000 gas balloons, 100 sideshows, eighty-six 'cosmoramic' theatres, thirty 'knock 'em downs' and Aunt Sallies, eight marionette theatres. There was no stinting on the food either – 30,000 meat pies, 30,000 slices of cake, 60,000 buns, 30,000 oranges and 9,000 gallons of lemonade and ginger beer. In attendance were 3,000 policemen, a squadron of Life Guards and ten Army water carts.

Treats figure in all the log books; not only the kind of treats which day and Sunday schools used shamelessly to bribe children to attend, but also the festivals and displays which the London School Board mounted with enthusiasm and a gift for public relations. These included the splendid concerts and music competitions at the Crystal Palace where over 4,000 children would sing supported by up to 250 instrumentalists from school orchestras, other concerts in the old Exeter Hall in the Strand, the Albert Hall and the old Queen's Hall, and drill demonstrations in Hyde Park and the Albert Hall where, among others, the Prince of Wales himself presented the prizes.

There were also the illicit pleasures, like the annual trip to Epsom for Derby day against which schools in south-west London fought a losing battle. 'The afternoon session was altered by a quarter of an hour in order to induce the children to attend school, the day being Derby day.' The Smallwood Road log for 9 November 1904 records the havoc caused by the death of Dan Leno, the music-hall comedian: 'A large number of children absent owing to the funeral at Lambeth Cemetery of Mr Dan Leno, the children in some cases being unable to pass the crowds of people.'

Social spectrum

The schools in the real slum areas kept log books preoccupied with poverty and its consequences. At the other end of the social scale, there were schools like the Fleet Road Board School, Hampstead, which built up a reputation as 'the Eton of the Board schools' because of its academic success and the way it began to attract a middle-class clientele. In 1896 this school contrived to win the top two scholarships for boys and the top two scholarships for girls out of 2,500 pupils in the L.C.C.'s competition. The *Daily Telegraph*, reporting this in awe, calculated that the nineteen scholarships won by the school in that year alone were worth '£871, which is the largest amount ever won by the scholars of one school in a twelve month'. Nevertheless, most of the junior classes even here were sixty-strong: one had 100 pupils, taught by one teacher and one pupil teacher.

Schools – and children – were clean or dirty according to their surroundings. Streets differed sharply from neighbouring streets. There was clean poverty and 'sordid, grimy, heart-rending poverty'. Teachers often had to tolerate the squalor they could not change. Dr P. B. Ballard's first school was at Settles Street on the borders of Whitechapel in 1885. 'I thought then, and I think now', he wrote, after half a century, 'that they needed soap and water much more than they needed pen, ink and paper.'

School meals

But many of the children needed food and clothing even more urgently than soap and water – the 'sickly complexions, pinched faces, emaciated limbs and other outward signs of the need of proper and regular nourishment' were there for all to see. Public funds could not legally be spent on school meals but again the school log books show how much the teachers themselves were involved in the voluntary and charitable efforts to relieve this kind of poverty through the agencies which provided clothing, and breakfasts and dinners for necessitous children.

Mrs E. M. Burgwin, headmistress of Orange Street School, Southwark, started to provide school dinners on a voluntary and charitable basis in the early 1880s with the aid of George R. Sims, the writer and drama critic. In 1889 the London School Dinner Fund was set up under the presidency of the Rev. J. R. Diggle, supported by a distinguished selection of the educational establishment including A. J. Mundella, M.P.

The teachers played a leading part in the voluntary efforts. For example in 1902, the East Lambeth Teachers' Association provided 38,000 dinners for needy children through a fund started in 1892 by the head of a Board school in Victory Place, Walworth – Mr W. H. Libby. Some idea of the mixture of sternness and kindliness which informed the charitable process can be gleaned from his own account of how he came to be involved in this work. Noticing two brothers in his school who seemed weak and languid, he asked if they were hungry. 'Yes Sir,' they replied, 'we have had nothing to eat for two days.' 'To test the truth of this statement, Mr Libby sent out for a pennyworth of the stalest bread that could be obtained; this he gave to the boys and they devoured it ravenously.' This it seems was enough to convince Mr Libby not only of their need, but of the needs of many others too, and the raising of funds began. As it happened, the principal benefactor turned out to be an ardent vegetarian and the 5,000 meals a day which came to be supplied had to be planned on strict vegetarian principles.*

Meanwhile the School Board set up an *ad hoc* Committee on Underfeeding which continued from year to year and encouraged the provision of meals. Argument turned on whether there should be free school dinners provided by the Board. The case for this was argued passionately when the Progressives returned to the control of the School Board in 1894 and Professor Graham Wallas became Chairman of the School Management Committee and its sub-committee on underfed children. It was a plank in the platform of the London Social Democratic Federation, and received the eloquent support of, among others, Mrs Bridges Adams, a Communist member. Even the tentative start, however, which Professor Wallas's Fabian tactics proposed, failed to engage the support of a majority of the members.

Schools of special difficulty

In 1884 the School Management Committee decided to introduce a special allowance for teachers in 'schools of special difficulty'. Head teachers got an extra £20 and assistants an extra £10. At first some fifteen schools were chosen, mainly in the worst of the central slums. To be considered for inclusion in the list, schools had to be those charging fees of not more than a penny a week, with many children leaving at the earliest possible opportunity, and with a transient school population.

* H. B. Philpott, *London at School*.

59

Of the fifteen schools which were included in the first list, five were in the Finsbury Division; Southwark had three, Hackney, Lambeth and Tower Hamlets two each, and one was in Greenwich.

As time went on the list was extended but the Board refused to consider any of the temporary schools for the special payments. As these included many of the worst schools, this undermined the effectiveness of the scheme, which was discontinued before the end of the School Board period.

From time to time, however, various schemes for special allowances for poor and difficult schools were operated under the L.C.C. before and after the First World War. The same principle was recommended by the Plowden Committee on Primary Education in 1967, and teachers in a number of London schools have qualified for the special 'educational priority area' allowance, since introduced by the Burnham Committee.*

Staffing and standards

Between 1872 and 1883 salaries were fixed in terms of a share of the grant earned by the pupils, plus a fixed salary paid by the Board. The Board's scheme was modified in 1875 to provide scales for men head teachers of £110–210 (£90–150 for women) and £55–110 (£50–90) for assistants. Graduates, male or female, received an extra £10. In 1883, the scales were revised and teachers ceased to have any direct share in the grant earned by their pupils. This was logical to get away from the odious principle of payment by results, but the Board was also influenced by the fact that heads of large schools were receiving more than had been intended—up to £700–800 a year which brought them close to the level of the Clerk of the School Board himself.

The new scale (besides introducing the payments for 'schools of special difficulty') gave heads £150–400 according to the size of their schools (£120–300 for headmistresses), while assistants' salaries ranged from £60 to £155 (£50–125). During the lifetime of the Board, the teaching staff built up from a mere 275 in 1875 to 11,601 in 1903, while the number of pupils per adult teacher dropped from 80·5 to 41·9. The build-up in the number of teachers was accompanied also by a steady improvement in their training and professionalism. By the end of the period the Board was recruiting 1,000 teachers a year including a sprinkling of graduates, as well as regularly taking the pick of the teachers coming out of the training colleges.

*See page 167.

The first Board in their enthusiasm – and foresight – had wished to found a central day training college, but no government grant was forthcoming and it was not legal for the Board to finance teacher training. After a succession of skirmishes with the Education Department and the District Auditor, the Board were allowed to bring the pupil teachers into special centres for a limited number of hours each week. These provided, in effect, a part-time secondary education for those products of the elementary system who had become apprenticed to teaching.* The first was established at Hackney in 1885 and eleven more followed in the next ten years. Given success in the Queen's scholarship examination at the end of their course, the pupil teacher could go on to training college.

With the improvement in staffing went an improvement in the results obtained by the schools, as measured by the standard examinations. As the final report of the Board noted, the life-cycle of the London Board can be divided neatly into three. The first ten years were marked by no perceptible progress in standards. It was as much as the school could do to contain the newly enrolled, often resentful boys and girls who stolidly resisted education. At the beginning they were heavily weighted at the bottom end of the standards – in 1874 over fifty-two per cent were below standard I.

The second decade began to show some real improvement – first in the three Rs, the three obligatory subjects in the H.M.I.'s examination. In the ten-year period, passes in arithmetic jumped by about eight percentage points, while those in writing rose by about six points and those in reading by about seven points. At the same time, the age-range within the schools began to change and the numbers in the upper standards began to rise.

From 1890 onwards the improvement became more rapid, as the expansion of the higher standard work already referred to began to be more marked. The Board tended to see the improvement in terms of an enlightened educational atmosphere – more children and families were becoming attuned to the idea of education and appreciation of what it could offer. It is also obvious, however, that the schools had become much more efficient teaching instruments, better staffed and equipped, in better buildings and that with these improvements had gone a major

* In his contribution to Spalding's book, Mr J. Nickal, an L.S.B. Inspector, felt constrained to point out that 'the students are largely drawn from the elementary schools and are of the social status so implied'. This was 1900. A measure of the importance of the social status of elementary school teachers can be gained from a recommendation in the Cross Report a little earlier (1888) that more 'women of superior social position and general culture' should be recruited as teachers. The first draft had defined them as 'ladies' which was more than the Commission could stomach and was duly amended.

readjustment in the standard which could be expected from 'the elementary school class of child'.

A significant consequence of the general rise in standard was the improved self-confidence of the teachers and their active professional association, the Metropolitan Board Teachers Association (a branch of the National Union of Elementary School Teachers) founded by George Collins in 1872. In the early period a number of London men were among the leaders of the N.U.E.T. – C. J. Addiscott, Robert Wild, G. Girling (who went on to become an L.S.B. inspector) and R. Sykes Collins, head of Clifton Road School, New Cross, was a lecturer on method at Borough Road College, editor of the *Schoolmaster* and served one three-year spell as a member of the London School Board.

Mr Tom Heller, first secretary of the National Union of Elementary Teachers, was a member of the Board from 1873 to 1888, returned as a Moderate. Other ex-teachers who served on the Board included Mr Henry Lynn (West Lambeth) and Mr G. Benson Clough (Finsbury) who were both Moderates, and Dr T. J. Macnamara (another editor of the *Schoolmaster* and M.P. for North Camberwell, a specialist in attacking Mr Diggle) and Thomas Gautrey on the Progressive benches.

The Board's inspectors were the main administrative officers with whom the schools came into contact. Till 1886 it was the rule for the Board's inspectors to give each school a thorough examination once a year, so that, with the H.M.I.'s visit, each school was inspected twice a year. The system began to break down as the number of Board schools grew and, rather than appoint a large number of additional inspectors, the Board decided to end the regular inspection and to limit these full-dress affairs to particular schools as necessary.

The inspectors had much to do which did not involve full inspection. They advised committees on all policy matters in the absence of a strong central administration. They were men of considerable importance and carried high prestige in the schools, though their salary was fixed during the first Board at only £300 a year, which was less than many head teachers were to earn. Powerful as the Board's inspectors were to influence policy and to make or mar the promotion prospects of individual teachers, they were minor figures compared with the H.M.I.s. These men occupied positions of real eminence, being appointed by the Queen and enjoying a measure of independence from the Education Department. They had complete control over the teachers who depended on them in two important respects.

EDUCATION  DEPARTMENT.

TEACHER'S CERTIFICATE OF THE SECOND CLASS.

Certificates of the Second Class are raised to the First Class by good service only.

THE LORDS OF THE COMMITTEE OF THE PRIVY COUNCIL ON EDUCATION

Hereby Certify That in the month of December, 1886

Louisa Jane Cox

having been a student during two years *in the*

Stockwell Training College .*was examined for a Certificate and placed in the* First *Division of Candidates of the* Second *Year.*

TWO YEARS
OF NORMAL TRAINING
SUCCESSFULLY
COMPLETED
DECEMBER 1886

Also That the above-named Candidate served the required period of probation in the New Kent Road Harper Street Board *School.*

In order that this Certificate may serve as evidence of Practical Success, it may, after every tenth Report entered upon it by H.M. Inspectors, be revised according to the character of the Reports.

Vice-President.

First Report.

Harper St. New Kent Roa .... *School visited on the* 4 *of* Dec 18 89

The grant was offered to this school this year without erasure under art 95 on the basis of excellence

H. M. Inspector.

Second Report.

.... *School visited on the* .... *of* .... 18 ....

H. M. Inspector.

(Over.)

R 2 3 (35,000s) 2000 12—86

A teacher's certificate (1889) showing the H.M.I.'s endorsement required to obtain salary increments.

First, success or failure in the examination meant more or less grant, and managers – even though the School Board might resolve otherwise – tended to use this as a measuring rod of the teacher's skill. And second, the teacher's personal dossier – his parchment – had to be endorsed each year by the H.M.I. with a grading and brief testimonial. To earn full salary, a teacher had to have ten satisfactory entries on his parchment. H.M.I. was, therefore, a figure of power in the teachers' lives, whose unannounced arrival was a matter of dread.

There was constant friction between the teachers' unions and the inspectorate, and especially with some of the parsons who remained inspectors of all schools after the separate category of clerical inspector came to an end with the 1870 Act. The man who contrived to acquire the bitterest hatred among the London teachers was the Rev. D. J. Stewart, who, whatever his other personal characteristics, seems to have delighted in humiliating small boys and girls and their unfortunate teachers. One of his classic tests for 6-year-olds in Greenwich as a dictation exercise was the sentence: 'If you twist that stick so long you will make your wrist ache.' Others used the most obscure sentences in order to find ways of confusing children with the phonetic ambiguities of the English language.

One of the tokens which marked the new regime at the Board under Sir George Kekewich was the retirement of Stewart on pension after a formal complaint from the teachers, led by W. J. Pope, the president of the N.U.E.T. This was regarded by Stewart as the teachers seeking their revenge – as indeed it was – but the episode, like the new-found willingness at the Education Department to consult with the teachers and recognize their union, indicated a stage which had been reached in the development of primary school teaching from the despised occupation of unqualified ushers into something more recognizably like a profession. Better training – in which London had played a part – was one element in this development. The N.U.E.T. was another. Teacher membership of the School Boards was a third. But with them went the organic growth of education itself and the dawning realization at the centre that this depended in large measure on the professional emancipation of the school master and school mistress.

Religious instruction

For most of the time religious instruction caused no particular difficulty. The Board had flexed its rules neatly in Whitechapel where a predominantly Jewish community wanted a Jewish headmaster and a minor crisis was averted by a little skilled diplomacy. Mr W. H. Smith's compromise worked well enough for twenty years. Trouble came at the end of 1892 when the Rev. J. J. Coxhead, who represented Marylebone from 1876 to 1897, visited a Board school where a scripture lesson was in progress. A child was asked who Jesus's father was and replied: 'Joseph'. (Coxhead, according to Thomas Gautrey, an arch-enemy of his on the Board, was alleged to pay the headmistress of his Church school only £40 a year and to combine a strong distaste for teachers' salaries with his devotion to religious teaching.)

As a result of this, the issue was taken up in February 1893 by Mr Athelstan Riley, member for Chelsea, a young barrister of High Church principles. He sought to persuade the Board to instruct teachers that they must give precise and orthodox explanations of the doctrine of the Incarnation and the Trinity. This was resisted by the majority but the Smith clause was amended to insert the word 'Christian' in front of 'morality and religion'. This seemingly innocent amendment was liable to have the same effect as Riley's more contentious motion, because it could force the School Board to do what the House of Lords was wisely chary of doing in the case of Bishop Colenso – interpret disputed Christian doctrine.

The debate lasted throughout 1893 and on till March 1894.* When more precise regulations were adopted, the teachers protested. Thomas Gautrey, their representative on the Board, presented an M.B.T.A. memorial signed by 3,130 of them demanding the withdrawal of the new rules and stating that they could not conscientiously continue to take Scripture unless this were done. The teachers and their union clearly recognized that, though for the most part they had always taught Christian religion and morality, once there was a threat to apply tests to this, they were at the mercy of the Board and the Inspectorate.

An attempt to make all teachers give a categorical 'yes' or 'no' to a direct question on their willingness to give religious teaching was postponed to allow tempers to cool. A mass meeting of 1,500 teachers pledged themselves to refuse. By this time the chairman of the Board, Mr Diggle, had come to see that he had made a mistake in backing Riley and Coxhead and with an election looming (which was to bring his chairmanship to an end) he allowed the matter to drop.

* Gautrey gives a graphic account of some of the late sittings towards the end when Riley rallied his supporters with oysters and Chablis.

Special schools

Before 1890, voluntary organizations had already made a start with schools for the blind, the deaf, the physically handicapped and the mentally subnormal. A Royal Commission on the Blind and Deaf sat from 1885 to 1889 and made major recommendations which formed the basis of legislation in 1893. This took the responsibility for the education of blind and deaf children away from the Poor Law Guardians and gave it to the school authority.

Much of the law was permissive only, leaving a great deal of initiative to the local school boards. Ten years before the Commission, London had appointed a peripatetic teacher for blind children in ordinary schools. A Miss Green was later appointed Superintendent, with two assistant instructresses, and instead of trying to teach blind children in ordinary elementary schools, the Board set up special centres which could be suitably equipped and where larger numbers could benefit from specialist instruction.

The Royal Commission gave added impetus to the development. By 1893 London had 156 blind children in twenty centres and six blind women were among the instructresses. To build up stronger units, children were boarded out in foster families if special centres were not available near their homes, and a new pattern was established for both blind and deaf children: day centres (where possible) up to the age of 13, followed by residential centres from 13 to 16 where vocational training could be given to help the boys and girls find jobs when they had to leave at 16.

At the beginning, the teaching of the deaf was based on a compromise between sign language and lip-reading. Within the first ten years lip-reading had won the day and ousted sign language except for the children whose hearing difficulties were the greatest.

The activities were on a small scale in relation to the need. The early pioneers of special education had to contend with strong prejudices, as well as the misguided kindness which could sap the self-reliance of their pupils. Inevitably, the mentally handicapped came at the end of the queue. The early procedures for 'ascertaining' children, and sending them to special schools where they would be boarded out, were inadequate and parental resistance was strong. Eventually in 1899 an Act was passed – the Elementary Education (Defective and Epileptic Children) Act – which gave the School Board power to compel parents to send children who had been 'ascertained' as in need of special education to the special school under threat of a £5 fine.

Much emphasis was placed on practical and trade instruction in all kinds of special school – basket work, typewriting and music for the blind; tailoring, shoemaking, wood and metal work for the deaf, and a variety of simple manual skills for the mentally handicapped.

To oversee the young people when they had to move outside the Board's responsibility at 16, care committees were set up which took a particular interest in trying to place them in employment. The L.S.B.'s sub-committee on blind and deaf children was set up in 1877 under the chairmanship of Sir Charles Reed, the second chairman of the Board. With the concurrence of the Education Department (but with no grant) the work continued till 1891 when the sub-committee's responsibilities were extended to take in the other physically and mentally handicapped.

As the Board's staff increased and the specialist organizers and staff were appointed, understanding both of what needed to be done and of what could be done was extended. By 1903 a working special school system had been established and was ready to turn over to the L.C.C. It consisted of four residential and ninety-one day schools (4,654 places) with six more residential schools and forty-one day schools at the planning stage. Teachers numbered 268 with eighty-eight other staff helpers, and the whole cost amounted to nearly £50,000 a year.

Evening schools

From the first there was an attempt to stretch the interpretation of the Elementary Education Act of 1870 to cover evening schools as well as day schools. First efforts came to nothing but during the 1880s a variety of evening classes were established. Some were to give elementary instruction under the Education Department's codes. Others, like those which gave rise to the Recreative Evening Schools Association, formed in 1885, widened the curriculum (on a self-supporting basis) by introducing subjects like cookery, wood-carving, physical training and music. Throughout the 1890s the numbers increased. Restrictions which had required a preliminary test in the three Rs were relaxed and fees (up to then averaging 3*d*. a week) were ended in 1898.

From 1893 onwards there was a separate code for evening continuation school and more liberal grants from the Education Department. It was already possible to discern separate strands in the thread of adult education: there were the cultural courses – 'the life and duties of a citizen', 'the reign of Queen Victoria illustrated by lantern slides of *Punch* cartoons' – (which appear to have evoked less than hoped for interest); there were the recreational activities for which there was clearly a demand, yet which appeared frivolous to the more ardent economists; and there were the solid vocational courses with more or less science, like those which earned grants from the Science and Art Department and helped to sustain the most serious evening work.

As the curriculum became more varied, so the institutions became more specialized. Some were organized as commercial schools where special attention was given to modern languages, shorthand, book-keeping, commercial law and similar subjects. Others were elevated to the status of Science and Art Schools, largely dependent upon grants from South Kensington.

As the century drew to an end it became more and more obvious that the confusion between the activities of the School Board and the Education Department on the one hand, and the Technical Education Board and the Science and Art Department on the other, had to be cleared up and, in spite of the fight put up by Lyulph Stanley, it became evident that the Technical Education Board would win.

The School Board had shown the extent of the need and had begun to meet it in a liberal manner which, while exposing the Board to attack, also ensured that when the responsibilities were unified in 1904, the new authority was forced to take a broad view of what comprised adult education. The result was to be seen in the rich combination of poly-technics and evening institutes on which London's further education service would come to be based.

5 School Board to County Council: the Technical Education Board, 1893-1904

It was in 1889 that Sir Charles Dilke successfully piloted his Local Government Act through Parliament and the major multipurpose units of local government which had been lacking in 1870 came into being. In the same year there was an indication of how they might ultimately come into conflict with the school boards. A Technical Instruction Act was passed which authorized the counties and county boroughs to raise a penny rate for technical and manual instruction.

The following year the link between the county and county borough councils and education was strengthened fortuitously but in the most effective way. In an attempt to encourage temperance a Bill was introduced raising duties on spirits. The original intention had been to use the revenue from this – expected to be about £750,000 – to compensate the licensed trade for the expected loss of business. Instead, Parliament responded to a brilliant opportunist campaign by Arthur Acland, the member who had promoted the Technical Instruction Act and 'a much underrated British statesman' in Beatrice Webb's phrase, and awarded the Whisky Money to the County Councils instead. Education was among the purposes to which the money could be put.

In London, the L.C.C. took no action on the permissive powers given under the Technical Instruction Act till 1892, when the second Council was elected and Sidney Webb and Quintin Hogg took the lead in proposing a special committee of inquiry to draw up a technical education scheme for London.

This was approved and Sidney Webb became chairman of the special committee. He held strong views on administration and his methods were very different from those adopted by the London School Board or, in other matters, by the L.C.C. Beatrice Webb spoke his mind in commenting in her diary: 'It is, perhaps, a sign that the County Council is still young that the whole direction of its administration is in the hands of the councillors and not relegated to paid servants. There are 20 or 30 men who make a profession of the Council.'

Webb was one who was prepared to devote a great deal of time to it, but he also believed in getting the best experts and letting them get on with it. The Special Committee, therefore, engaged Mr Herbert Llewellyn Smith, one of Acland's former lieutenants, to survey the resources for technical education in the metropolis and make recommendations. His report was ready within a year. Technical education in London, he said, 'is not only far behind Germany and France in quantity and quality, but also far behind our chief provincial towns'. To illustrate this he quoted the example of Manchester where evening class numbers in technical subjects had more than doubled to 14,000 since Acland's Act. 'To be on a level with Manchester there should be 140,000 entries in corresponding classes in London instead of the 24,000 revealed in the survey.'

Llewellyn Smith, who had served as a research assistant to Charles Booth in his survey of *London Life and Labour*, included in his report an analysis of London employment showing how manufacturing industry was distributed. Certain trades were still closely associated with particular localities – the building trades with south and west London and Hackney in the north-east, the metal trades in Poplar and Greenwich in the east, wood and furniture trades in Shoreditch and Bethnal Green, printing and bookbinding in Holborn and Southwark, chemical trades in the St Olave Ward of Southwark, clothing trades for men and boys in the City and for women and girls in Shoreditch and Bethnal Green.

He recommended a policy which combined a generous system of junior and senior scholarships to help elementary school pupils to go on to more advanced courses, and a programme of grants to support work in the secondary and technical schools and polytechnics. Implicit in this was a wide interpretation of technical education which was not restricted to technological or scientific applications but, as Sidney Webb observed later, came to cover any subject except Greek and theology. The teaching resources were widely interpreted, also, to include not merely technical institutes but all secondary schools and colleges (including those coming under the aegis of London University examinations) offering courses in arts subjects, science and technology and technical studies.

On the basis of this report and the programme it set out, costed at £85,000 for the first year, the L.C.C. set up a Technical Education Board with Sidney Webb as chairman. It consisted of twenty councillors and fifteen members nominated or coopted. This reflected another of Webb's ideas – that it was often more effective to work through existing bodies than to set up a large new administrative machine. The London School Board, the London Trades Council and the City and Guilds of London Institute each had three representatives. Two were nominated by the City Parochial Charities, one each by the National Union of Teachers and the Head Masters Association; two were coopted by the Board.

The man chosen as first and only secretary of the Technical Education Board was Dr William Garnett, a formidable university administrator ('William the Builder') who had built up first the Nottingham University College and then the Durham College of Science at Newcastle, and who at forty-three was at the height of his energetic powers.

Working closely with Webb he set about putting the Llewellyn Smith policies into operation. The junior county scholarship scheme was the first priority, to help thirteen-year-olds from elementary school get to the secondary schools and schools of science. These were the new scholarships which began to appear on elementary school honour boards, alongside the 1,000 or so scholarships of £5 and upwards currently being awarded by more than 100 charities and foundations and by the Science and Art Department. As a start it was decided to award an additional 500 junior county scholarships for 1893, amounting to fees plus £10 a year maintenance 'intended to compensate parents to some extent for the loss of earnings which their children might otherwise obtain'.

By 1903 this had been increased to 600 and 100 intermediate scholarships had been added for pupils of 16–19, forty-five senior scholarships and exhibitions, thirty art scholarships and 800 other awards for various kinds of technical instruction.

Dr Garnett was a man who worked with the minimum of clerical assistance – he managed with an assistant, Dr Bernard Allen (later deputy education officer to Sir Robert Blair at the L.C.C.), whose expertise was in secondary education, a full-time domestic economy expert, Miss Ella Pycroft, a part-time Inspector, Dr C. W. Kimmins, who advised on laboratory provision, two distinguished art advisers, George (later Sir George Frampton and W. R. Lethaby, and six clerks.

Frampton was a sculptor, now remembered for (among other work) three well-known London statues – Quintin Hogg in Portland Place, Edith Cavell near St Martin-in-the-Fields and Peter Pan in Kensington Gardens. Lethaby was the man who created the Central School of Arts and Crafts and (according to Dr Allen) 'did more to raise the standard of craft teaching in London than any other man'.

In addition to the scholarship scheme there were the grants to secondary schools and technical institutes. The Parochial Charities and City companies had made a start with grants of over £50,000 a year to institutions such as the Regent Street Polytechnic and other polytechnic institutes. In ten years, the number of these institutes increased to twenty-six, while day classes trebled and evening students multiplied by four. Among the new institutions set up with support from the Technical Education Board there was the London Day Training College (later the London University Institute of Education), the Central School of Arts and Crafts and specialist monotechnics for photography and photoengraving, carriage building, typography and printing, leather dying and tanning and the furniture trades. With the aid of T.E.B. grants, fifty laboratories, eighteen workshops and twenty-five lecture rooms were added to existing secondary schools and the standards of teaching raised at the same time.

Garnett's shoe-string administration enabled complicated schemes to go ahead at great speed with the bare minimum of bureaucratic interference. Dr Allen recalled how Garnett's all-round ability enabled him to be his own expert and take on the craftsmen at their own trade:

In matters where other men might have wanted to call in the help of an engineer or a surveyor or a valuer or a financier, he took on the job himself with the minimum of delay. . . . No sooner did the idea arise, for instance, of putting up a technical school in a given area than he set to work himself to plan the adaptation of an existing building, drew up the specification for the required equipment and sketched the programme of work for the instructors to follow.

Within four years of starting the job he had opened five new polytechnics, set up the Central School, founded three new technical institutes and provided laboratories and equipment for science teaching at forty secondary schools.

Webb was the ideal chairman for Garnett because, as well as bringing to the job remarkable political and persuasive gifts ('"Wily Webb" as Sidney is called') and a dispatch of business almost as rapid as Garnett's, if more conventional, he had a firm grasp of the larger educational aims. He was interested in technical education (as currently defined) but he was more interested in creating a public education system which would link all the separate kinds of education in a well-adjusted whole.

This aim led Webb to work with Haldane on the reform of London University. They both believed it could no longer continue as an institution solely concerned with providing examinations for students in teaching colleges. Instead Webb wanted a teaching university organized by faculties, with student life based on a number of collegiate institutions – full- and part-time – some autonomous, others provided by public authorities; while at the same time insisting on the retention of the external London degree and the opportunities it represented for part-time students everywhere.

> What was essential [wrote Mrs Webb] was to have in view from the first, and to work steadily towards it, though not necessarily talk about it, a scheme of education for London as a whole, in which all grades and kinds of formal education, from the kindergarten to the university, in all subjects, and at all colleges, would find an appropriate place and be duly coordinated and connected.

In a penetrating passage (in an article in the *Nineteenth Century*, June 1902) Webb caught the strength and weakness of the collegiate system.

> So long as the several colleges and other teaching institutions regard themselves and are regarded as the units of university organization [he wrote], their instinctive megalomania is a disruptive force, creating internecine jealousy and competition for students and impelling each particular institution, irrespective of its local conditions or special opportunities to strive to swell itself into a complete university on a microscopic scale. Make the faculty the unit and the same megalomania . . . serves only to enhance the reputation of the university as a whole. . . .

It was as a result of reform on these lines – ratified in 1900 – that some of the London polytechnics and other major institutions aided by the Technical Education Board became recognized as 'schools of the university' and able to present candidates for internal degrees. In an ideal world, Webb's comprehensive approach might have been extended further inside London and outside to provide organic links between the public and the autonomous sectors in higher education, had not the infusion of central government finance via the University Grants Committee ensured that civic universities should become national institutions, and the 'instinctive megalomania' which Webb ascribed to colleges proved to be a quality of sectors within the system as well as of individual units.

Webb's quest for a unified system of education for London also determined his attitude to the controversy up to the 1902 Education Act, in which he played an important part behind the scenes. There were many ingredients to the dispute. There was the need to create an administrative mechanism to enable secondary education to be brought within the public system. There was the need sooner rather than later to bring the non-provided elementary schools into a more regular relationship with the Board schools and to provide them with local financial assistance.

For the most part the school boards – which numbered more than 2,000 – were too small and there were many areas without a board at all. Moreover, they were associated with a hostile attitude towards voluntary schools and it was popularly supposed that as *ad hoc* bodies they were too heavily influenced by special interests within education such as teachers' unions.

In an abortive Bill in 1896 a move had been made to give new educational duties for secondary education to the counties and county boroughs. It failed to last the parliamentary course, but the ideas behind it – including the suggestion that elementary schools should be restricted to more clearly defined elementary work while the functions being taken on by higher grade schools might more properly belong to secondary and technical schools – indicated the lines along which thinking was moving.

In 1897 the Science and Art Department *Directory* contained a new clause, VII, the upshot of which was to invite county councils (in the case of London, the Technical Education Board) to coordinate grants from the Science and Art Department. This was taken at the time to be a challenge to the school boards who were financing a large part of the ex-standard work in their higher grade schools from Science and Art funds and who were debarred from spending rate funds on secondary education.

For a while the London Technical Education Board did nothing. Its membership included representatives of the School Board led by Lyulph Stanley who argued vehemently against the Technical Education Board, in the words of the Science and Art Department's minute, notifying 'its willingness to be responsible to the Department for the Science and Art instruction in its area'. But in 1898 the decision to do so was taken. The conflict between the Technical Education Board and the School Board became more intense – with sharp disagreements among the members of the Progressive Party who controlled both bodies – and the School Board appealed for a formal hearing by the Science and Art Department at South Kensington to resolve the dispute. This was set for 1 February 1899.

It was at this point that Robert Morant in the Education Department took a hand. He had joined the Department in 1895 after a career in the Far East and worked with Sadler in the Office of Special Inquiries and Reports. In 1897 he had been appointed joint secretary of a departmental committee set up to look into the relationship between higher grade schools and secondary schools. He rapidly formed the view that much of the School Board activity in the development of higher grade schools and evening schools was illegal and involved the expenditure of public money *ultra vires*. But Sir George Kekewich, his official head, was strongly in favour of this development and was sympathetic towards the school boards.

It was for this reason that Morant employed his stratagem of planting a paragraph in an otherwise innocuous report on education in Switzerland which suggested in as many words that

Many School Boards have decided to improve their higher elementary education . . . by providing day schools of higher grade; but they have frequently been told by the Central Authority that they cannot take any such steps as could involve the School Board in any expense for this purpose, that it would be illegal to spend their rates in such a manner, inasmuch as they were only empowered by the Act of 1870 to use the rates to provide Elementary Education.

With this he supplied a series of references to cases reported in the *School Board Chronicle*.

In practice, the school boards had recently been spending rate funds on 'non-elementary' education with the connivance and encouragement of Sir George Kekewich, but this did not prevent Morant from getting in touch with Garnett and, in conditions of strictest secrecy on Boxing Day 1898, briefing Garnett's assistant Bernard Allen with the references on which to build the Technical Education Board's case for the forthcoming inquiry which Sir John Donnelly, Secretary of the Science and Art Department, was to conduct.

Sir John Gorst was present as an observer at the hearing on 1 February 1899, when Sir John Donnelly had no hesitation in ruling in favour of the T.E.B. After a meeting with Donnelly and Kekewich, Gorst and Garnett planned a test case before the District Auditor to challenge the legal position of the London School Board.

There were technical difficulties – the Board was only obliged to give a complainant the minimum of assistance and the accounts were voted in such a manner as to make it hard to disentangle one controversial payment from many others which raised no query. Eventually it was discovered that the Camden School of Art was incorporated and could put in an appearance as a rate-payer through professional representatives. Mr Francis Black, the principal, and one of the Governors, Mr Hales, a solicitor, duly made a formal complaint.

The upshot was a decision by the Auditor, Mr T. Barclay Cockerton, against the School Board (July 1899) which was subsequently upheld in the High Court and in the Court of Appeal. A short Act was brought in to legitimate London's activities pending the new major 1902 Education Act. Morant was made Cabinet adviser in the preparation of the Bill behind Kekewich's back in circumstances which defy brief description but combined low farce with top-level intrigue. His influence also replaced that of Gorst, the management of the 1902 Bill being taken over by the Prime Minister, Mr Arthur Balfour. Sidney Webb had by now stepped down from the chair of the T.E.B., but in her diary Beatrice Webb conveys a graphic description of Morant's indiscreet conversation giving

glimpses into the work of one department of English Government. The Duke of Devonshire, the nominal Education Minister, failing through inertia and stupidity to grasp any complicated detail half an hour after he has listened to the clearest exposition of it, preoccupied with Newmarket, and in bed till 12 o'clock, Kekewich trying to outstay this Government and quite superannuated in authority, Gorst cynical and careless having given up even the semblance of any interest in the office; the Cabinet absorbed in other affairs and impatient and bored with the whole question of education.

'Impossible to find out after a Cabinet meeting,' Morant tells us, 'what has actually been the decision. Salisbury doesn't seem to know or care, and the various Ministers who do care, give out contradictory versions.'

Under the 1902 Act – which did not apply to London – the counties and county boroughs became the local education authorities, though non-county boroughs were allowed to exercise powers in elementary education. London was the subject of a separate Bill the following year, surrounded by more intrigue in the dying years of the Conservative Government. There were intrigues between the School Board which hoped to be nominated as the authority for all London education and the Technical Education Board which favoured the London County Council (of which the T.E.B. was a Committee). Sidney Webb and Ramsay MacDonald intrigued energetically against each other on the L.C.C. There were divisions also among the politicians. Some distrusted the School Board because it was *ad hoc* and thought liable to be dominated by teachers and parsons; others feared the L.C.C. because it was too big and had a large progressive majority; yet others flirted with handing education over to the Metropolitan boroughs and breaking up the London School Board area. Close parallels can be drawn between this last scheme of which Mr Walter Long was a proponent and the proposals for the reorganization of London education following the Herbert Commission in 1960, which was defeated by the combined efforts of the L.C.C. education committee and the Ministry of Education. Others wanted a scheme for education similar to the Metropolitan Water Board which would create an *ad hoc* authority without direct election, not wholly unlike that evolved for the Inner London Education Authority some sixty years later.

Sidney Webb had as much as anyone to do with the decision – reflected in the London Education Bill, 1903 – to transfer education lock, stock and barrel to the L.C.C., pulling wires skilfully among the conservative politicians at Westminster and among the members of both the L.C.C. and the London School Board and feeding *The Times*, *Morning Post* and *Daily Mail* with ammunition in favour of the Bill.

The Bill became an Act and the whole of London's public educational enterprise – Board schools, Church schools, special schools, continuation schools, evening schools, art schools, technical institutes, polytechnics – was brought together under the authority of the London County Council. But not before Dr William Garnett had damaged his own professional career by showing an M.P. a confidential memorandum setting out his suggested scheme for the L.C.C.'s administration of education. The document found its way into *The Times* office and became public, thus compromising Garnett and the L.C.C. The consequence may well have had a marginal effect in helping to pass the Bill. Beyond any doubt it prejudiced Garnett who was cold-shouldered when the time came for the L.C.C. to take over and, as Education Adviser, kept out of any executive office in the new administration.

Part two *1904-44*

6 L.C.C. takes over

After all the wrangling, the change-over from the London School Board to the London County Council went remarkably smoothly. The Progressives, whom Webb had accused of being more concerned to spite the Government than to look to the welfare of the schools, were in control of the L.C.C. as they had been of the London School Board. In spite of political opposition and general hostility to the religious settlement which was giving rise elsewhere to passive resistance, they pitched in with energy, under the leadership of Sir William Collins, first chairman of the Education Committee, to the reorganization which the Act demanded.

Domestically, the first task was to bring education within the administrative structure of the County Council. The intention was to maintain a unified administration with as few watertight compartments as possible, led by the clerk of the Council, Mr G. L. Gomme, in the position of *primus inter pares*.

Within the education department there were the difficulties to be expected during the early period in which the separate administrations of the School Board and the Technical Education Board had to be welded together. Dr William Garnett, a man of outstanding and proven ability as the former secretary to the Technical Education Board, was still only 53. But even had he not been indiscreet and incurred the wrath of many councillors before the Education Committee took over, it is doubtful if his individualistic administrative style would have been suitable for the organization of a large staff. He was, therefore, appointed Education Adviser, while the post of Executive Officer of the Education Department went to Mr Robert Blair. Dr Bernard Allen, Garnett's former assistant, was appointed to take charge of higher education, becoming Blair's deputy in 1907. Dr C. W. Kimmins, ex-Chief Inspector of the T.E.B., was appointed Chief Inspector.

The third member of the senior team, Mr H. J. Mordaunt, came from the Board of Education. He was appointed chief clerk and attached to the Clerk's department to emphasize the unified administration of the Council. The *troika* arrangement did not take long to break down. As Sir Harry Haward, who later became Comptroller of the L.C.C. from 1920 to 1930, recalled, 'this unusual arrangement, dictated partly by personal considerations, soon produced a crop of difficulties . . . which ultimately resolved themselves on the personal side into a battle royal between the Clerk of the Council and the Executive Officer'.* By the summer of 1907 the L.C.C. General Purposes Committee had to sort out the difficulties and to make new proposals.

The result was that the education service was recognized to be different in its character from the other municipal services, and in the nature of the administrative and professional advice which it demanded. A new position of Education Officer was created and Robert Blair (who was knighted in 1914) was given the responsibility of pulling the whole administrative organization together, thus doing away with the artificial separation of administration from professional advice. Garnett's appointment was redefined and he became solely an advisory and intelligence officer, while the Clerk to the Council ceased to be responsible for minuting the Education Committee meetings. Garnett's office lapsed when he retired in 1915.

The episode is not without interest in view of later discussions of management in local government. During the Second World War the Clerk's department again took over the minuting of education committees, an arrangement which has continued.

Robert Blair was a formidable Scot. He was born in 1859 in Wigtown, educated at the local village school and, after a spell as a pupil teacher in Edinburgh, came to London in 1882 to teach science at Aske's Hatcham, one of London's endowed schools where one of the men who later succeeded him, E. M. Rich, was among his pupils. After a short spell as principal of a school of science at Cheltenham, he was recruited to the Science and Art Department's inspectorate and – a reminder that this department's writ also ran north of the border – was responsible for inspecting technical and higher education in the north district – from Dumfries to Lerwick.

During the four years immediately before being appointed in London he served in Ireland as an Assistant Secretary in the Department of

* *The London County Council from Within* by Sir Harry Haward.

Agriculture and Technical Education, helping to set up a network of local technical schools. This led to an invitation to join a commission of inquiry sponsored by a millionaire engineer by the name of Moseley, which visited the United States to test one of Moseley's theories – that American education produced better engineers than the English system. Blair wrote a report on his return, *Some Features of American Education*, which was predictably critical of much American practice but drew attention to the contrast in social attitudes. (When the L.C.C. came to prepare the 1947 school plan, Blair's report was taken out and searched for prescient insights which might be said to point towards comprehensive schools. It was not particularly helpful on this score, but two of his fellow-travellers were L.C.C. councillors, and the contacts which he made on the Moseley Commission indirectly helped to bring his name forward for the executive position in 1904.)

For the next twenty years, Blair was to be the dominant force in educational policy making for London. Rich described him as 'a magnificent fighter'. He had 'a magnificent leonine head', white hair and a long aquiline nose. His platform manner was impressive – 'his beautiful speech, once described by Sir Henry Newbolt as his ideal' was one of his great assets. This was backed up by a forceful personality – 'at times . . . direct almost to the point of harshness' – which gave London the kind of educational leadership it had never had from a professional chief before.

The broad lines on which the London school system was to develop over the next forty years were firmly established during the years between 1904 and the outbreak of the First World War.

Under Blair's lead, the L.C.C. had to take up the responsibilities which the 1902 Education Act had given to local education authorities, some mandatory, some permissive. As the Metropolitan authority, always conscious of national and imperial obligations, London was keenly aware that a lead had to be given to others. Each volume of *The London Education Service* (the authority's official manual) between 1905 and 1939 included a paragraph which emphasized this:

London is the home of the world's markets; the centre of international finance; the capital city of a world-wide Empire; the meeting place of nearly every race and people. It is not only, therefore, the needs of the 'locality' which are insistent on their claim on the London Education Authority. The policy of London, including the organization of its education service, must be largely influenced by Imperial circumstances and the general advance of humanity. For it is on these that its own existence largely depends.

It would be a mistake to lose sight of this sense of greatness, nor yet to suppose that, because of the sharpness of the contrast between this imperial grandiloquence and the contemporary picture of poverty and pathos in the riverside slums, there was something false about it. What is true beyond a doubt is that most people found little difficulty in accepting the poverty, malnutrition, infant mortality and educational backwardness of the poorer classes as part of the natural order of things like the Empire itself, or the class system.

In strictly relative terms, the evidence of progress was there for all to see as a rapidly increasing number of boys and girls were being caught up in the educational machine. But this sense of rapid improvement made it easy to understate the darker side. When in the South African war, and in both world wars, evidence was revealed of ignorance and poor child health and physique and the limited penetration of education as a social force in the lives of the children of the slums, it came as a shock to compare the complacent pride in real achievement with the facts of life on London's underside.

A major task for the new L.C.C. Education Committee was to integrate the Board schools and the 'non-provided' schools into a single coordinated system. The L.C.C. took over 521 Board schools attended by an average of 485,000 pupils. To these were now added 438 voluntary schools with another 175,000 pupils. Not only, as the figures show, were the voluntary schools much smaller than the Board schools, they were also much less well housed, equipped and staffed and the annual cost per pupil at £2 9s. 3d. worked out at only about half the £4 15s. 9d. a year spent on each pupil in the schools provided by the authority.

The most urgent need was to carry out a survey of buildings and instruction similar to that undertaken in 1871. This meant strengthening the inspectorate to carry this out and to administer the larger network of schools. In February 1905 the Council accepted plans for a new organization: instead of operating with eight district inspectors and thirteen sub-inspectors, there were to be four divisional inspectors 'of high academic distinction', assisted by twelve district inspectors and twelve assistant inspectors. In addition there were three specialist inspectors for art, women's classes and metal work.

While the survey was being carried out, the voluntary schools were maintained on a provisional basis and the normal benefits enjoyed by council schools were progressively applied to them. They were brought into the underfed children's scheme, relieved of fees for manual training centres, supplied with cupboards and apparatus, and included in the authority's prize competitions. All the schools adopted the same educational year ending at the close of the summer term. An early warning was issued that the monitorial system would have to end.

The survey showed how much the non-provided school buildings left to be desired by the standards of the School Board (and Technical Education Board) which had been adopted, as appropriate, by the L.C.C. Ninety-two schools were found to be unsuitable for educational purposes. Some were 'so badly and flimsily built' that it was better to build a new school than to make improvements. Others lacked adequate sanitation or were structurally unsafe; roofs leaked, playgrounds were inadequate; there were fire hazards. In some 314 schools the drains were condemned.

An immediate building and renovation programme was launched. Managers were told to improve the lighting, heating and ventilation, lay on drinking water, improvise a staff room, paint and decorate, remove galleries and stepping in old classrooms.* Many schools were overcrowded on the regulation basis of one square yard in infant classes. In others, declining school rolls meant they were over-staffed and needed to be reorganized on a more rational basis.

Less than three years later (in March 1908) Blair could report that seventy-nine schools had closed or were about to close, 210 were by now satisfactory; in 104 cases renovation had begun, four had become council schools and others had asked for extra time.

All this placed heavy burdens on the voluntary school authorities as the price of the relief from responsibility for running expenses. In one respect the new education authority felt cheated. Under Section 13 of the Act, London had hoped to become entitled to some of the endowment income which went with the non-provided schools. This income was believed to amount to £29,000 a year and, on this basis, the L.C.C. Education Committee Report for 1906 estimated the endowments themselves were worth £950,000. Not surprisingly the Council regarded the £6 12s. it had managed to lay hold on in the first two years a poor return in the circumstances.

The survey of the teaching in the non-provided schools was more encouraging than the survey of buildings: only nine per cent of the schools were found to be completely unsatisfactory and it was reported that 'considering the condition of many of the schools, the results were remarkable'. But whereas in the ex-Board schools ninety-eight per cent of the

Forty years later, the post-1944 Act L.C.C. was still busy removing stepping. See p. 148.

12,000 teachers held certificates, only fifty-one per cent of the 4,400 voluntary school teachers were certificated. In both categories of school many of the teachers who held certificates had only obtained them on the basis of qualification by experience, not by a training college course.

In response to this, a large-scale programme of in-service training was set up. Uncertificated teachers were given the opportunity to take courses, and to gain their certificates by part-time study. The younger staff were encouraged to enter a training college to take one or two years of professional training. At the same time salary scales were improved with a fifteen per cent rise for the maximum of the assistant teachers' scale to £200 a year. By 1914, ten years after the voluntary schools had come under the L.C.C., some ninety-three per cent of all the permanent staff in these schools were certificated.

In addition to crash programmes aimed at training unqualified teachers, the education authority had set up a regular service of lectures and courses to raise the standard of elementary school teaching throughout the London schools. Celebrities such as Gilbert Murray, Sir Henry Newbolt and Sir Arthur Keith were among those who gave courses. In 1908–9 it was estimated that over 7,000 teachers took part in university classes at Saturday and evening sessions. This remained a feature of the L.C.C. programme, though in an economy drive fees were introduced to cover the cost after the First World War.

A year later a 'library for the circulation of books among those engaged in the work of London education' was set up because, in Blair's words,

to achieve the best results in the training of its future citizens, it is important that the Council should do all it can to keep its teachers in touch with the latest developments of educational theory and should also give them facilities for pursuing their knowledge of other subjects.

This was the beginning of the Education Library now housed on the fourth floor at County Hall, containing volumes at the disposal of London teachers and educational administrators. Books were also circulated by the public libraries on a divisional basis. Public libraries in Bethnal Green, Greenwich, Poplar, Islington, Stoke Newington, Battersea, Camberwell and Holborn were among those who joined in by setting up juvenile lending departments.

As for the teachers themselves, their methods, talents and limitations were what might be expected from the way they were recruited and trained and the impossible tasks they faced. Most of them had started as monitors at 14, progressing by way of part-time pupil-teacher centres and, if they were lucky, the Queen's Scholarship, to training colleges where the regime was narrow in the extreme. They combined a powerful and often savage discipline with systematic instruction for standards prescribed in detail by the Codes.

The new vision of what the elementary school could be, set out in the preface of the 1904 Code, remained an expression of the ideal – liberal in tone, and commending a relatively broad elementary course. In a paragraph of direct importance to the new local education authorities, the Code insisted that

it will be an important, though subsidiary object of the school to discover individual children who show promise of exceptional capacity, and to develop their special gifts (so far as this can be done without sacrificing the interests of the majority of the children) so that they may be qualified to pass at the proper age into secondary schools and be able to derive the maximum of benefit from the education there offered to them.

The increase in the number of junior county scholarships began to make an impact on the elementary schools during the first decade of the century. The attitudes of teachers and pupils differed widely from one area to another. Scholarships were available for less than five in every 100 children. What Fleet Road, Hampstead, could take in its stride would be exceptional in Southwark or Tower Hamlets. Social distinctions between streets and the schools which served them could still remain sharp in places like Fulham where povery and relative prosperity jostled side by side. Eric Walker, who went on to become borough education officer for Bedford, has written of his own journey up the London scholarship ladder before and during the First Word War. He recalls that several of his cleverest contemporaries refused the proffered scholarships, because their parents could not afford to do without juvenile earnings, or for the simpler but no less obstructive reason that they regarded secondary schools as serving a different social group from ordinary people like them.

Writing in 1909, an L.C.C. assistant inspector, Dr F. H. Hayward, commented on ' an absence of interest in the psychological aspects of the art of teaching' among the elementary school staff:

This absence [he believed] is indicated correctly in the paucity of educational journals in England as compared with the several hundred issued yearly in Germany, and by the marked superiority in philosophical grasp of American books on education over English. Within the schools this defect is indicated by the sinister absence of any controversy over fundamental principles; teachers do not array themselves under the banners of this or that 'educationist' or swear allegiance to this or that psychological doctrine; such controversies as arise in their ranks are usually generated *ab extra*. . . . Such psychology as prevails is an antiquated doctrinairianism that talks glibly about training this or that 'faculty'; and none of the recent advances in the science – important and practical though they are – have yet seriously influenced the schools. . . . The situation appears to be saved (as is so often the case in English affairs) by the existence of the high level of traditional, though empirical efficiency.*

It seems that Dr Hayward was not alone in recognizing the importance of developments in educational psychology. In 1913 Dr Cyril Burt was appointed as part-time educational psychologist to the L.C.C. Education Committee, the first such appointment in the country. He drew up his own remit – to carry out psychological surveys of the children in L.C.C. schools, to examine and report on individual cases of educational subnormality, individual gifted children, and on delinquency, and to study and report on the psychological aspects of specific educational problems such as entrance and scholarship qualifications.

No less important than the integration of the non-provided and ex-School Board elementary schools, was the union in the Education Committee of the separate functions hitherto exercised by school boards and (in London) the Technical Education Board. This included, among other things, the need to develop a policy for secondary education. Where others were limited to spending a twopenny rate on 'higher education', as this activity was called, London had no statutory limit.

From the T.E.B., the Council inherited a scholarship scheme and a £42,000-a-year programme of grants-in-aid to about fifty schools. From the School Board it inherited a range of higher grade schools, many of which aspired to secondary status, but which had been effectively hobbled by Morant in the closing years of the School Board.

Morant lost no time in establishing what he meant by a secondary school by setting down the official view in a memorandum attached to regulations issued in 1904. Secondary schools had to provide courses which were 'general' – i.e. not specialized or pre-vocational – and 'complete', leading to a definite standard at the end of the course at 16 plus. The regulations went on to lay down what the course should provide:

* For an echo nearly sixty years later, see *Curriculum Innovation in Practice*. A Report of the Third International Curriculum Conference, 1967, London: H.M.S.O. Except that some of the confidence in 'empirical efficiency' had evaporated.

English language, and literature, at least one language other than English, Geography, History, Mathematics, Science and Drawing with due provision for manual work and physical exercise, and in a girls' school for housewifery. Not less than $4\frac{1}{2}$ hours per week must be allotted to English, Geography and History; not less than $3\frac{1}{2}$ hours to the language where only one is taken or less than 6 hours when two are taken; and not less than $7\frac{1}{2}$ hours to Science and Mathematics, of which at least 3 must be for Science. The instruction of Science must be both theoretical and practical. When two languages other than English are taken and Latin is not one of these, the Board will require to be satisfied that the omission of Latin is for the advantage of the school.

This was the original pattern, firmly linked with the traditional grammar school and ensuring that the new county grammar schools were founded on this model and not on the higher grade schools or the schools of science developed by the grants of the former Science and Art Department.

London immediately embarked on an extensive programme of action to increase the number of secondary school places available. This was not just because of the energy or guile of Sidney Webb, who again appeared at a critical juncture to take the chair of the Higher Education Committee. A rapid expansion of secondary education was part of Morant's plan; he was determined to end the pupil-teacher system and to recruit intending teachers from the grammar schools. This was essential if the closed circle of the elementary school system was to be broken.

The first step which Sidney Webb took was to get the Council to agree to an increase in the number of junior county scholarships to 2,000 a year.* At the same time the scholarship age was reduced to 11 and the examination itself was simplified to a test of arithmetic and English intended 'to test intelligence rather than acquired knowledge'. Some of the awards were known as 'probationers' scholarships' and continued to be made at 13 with the aim of encouraging potential teachers. But an earlier proposal to earmark scholarships at 11 against a promise to enter teaching was rejected by the Council with outraged references to 'child-slavery'.

When it was argued that this was too ambitious because there were not enough secondary school places to take this number of scholars, Webb replied: 'Let the Council appoint the full 2,000: we will find schools for them'.

The main difficulty was to find sufficient schools for the girls. The endowed schools were mainly boys' schools. In a modest way the Endowed

* Actually 2,167 awards were made, but twenty per cent left their grammar schools by the age of 14.

Schools Commissioners, and later the Charity Commissioners, had helped to redress the balance by enabling some girls' schools to be founded in the later nineteenth century by the rationalization of charitable endowments. But more than these were needed to ensure a supply of girls into teacher training – and if the 2,000 scholarships were to be awarded.

Dr Bernard Allen has described how the 2,000 places were found during the summer of 1905:

> By hunting all over London we managed to pick up seven buildings either already used as schools or shortly to be opened, which we secured for conversion into 'County Secondary Schools'. . . . It was decided that all these new county schools should be girls' schools. Advertisements were accordingly issued for seven headmistresses, and the Board Room was thronged with candidates when the Committee at a prolonged sitting selected the whole of the seven.

The first batch of schools included Kingsland, Manor Mount, Sydenham and Fulham. The Grocers' Company transferred Hackney Downs Grammar school to the L.C.C. The Estate Governors of Alleyn's College of God's Gift at Dulwich offered a site, and other schools were planned at Woolwich, Hackney, Fulham, Chelsea, Clapham and Wandsworth.

Altogether, in all London's secondary schools, including the private schools and public schools not receiving grant aid, there were about 11,000 places in 1904. It was reckoned that by 1910–11, when the Council's full scholarship scheme had fully come into operation, about 11,000 places would be required for scholars alone. It was expressly provided that all schools used by the L.C.C., including the county secondary schools, should have a mixture of scholarship-holders and fee-payers to help create a social balance (in the case of the county schools the original intention was to have sixty per cent scholars and forty per cent fee-payers). By 1907 the number of county secondary schools had risen to sixteen and the number of extra places to 4,000, most of them for girls. By the same date it was estimated that expansion of the aided schools had added another 2,000.

By 1919 the county secondary schools numbered twenty-three, with 8,072 pupils of whom 2,653 were boys and 5,419 were girls. There were by then more than 28,000 other places in aided and independent schools. Thus, in the fifteen years after 1904, the total number of secondary places in London had been effectively trebled under the stimulus of grants-in-aid and scholarships from the local authority and the additional grants paid by the Board of Education. A new set of secondary school regulations, introduced by the Board in 1907, raised the capitation grant on each pupil between the ages of 12 and 18 to £5 in schools which guaranteed to provide twenty-five per cent of places free of fees.

At the same time, the curriculum was developing. F. S. Boas, one of the L.C.C. divisional inspectors, writing in 1910, commented on the way in which the tendency to specialize in sciences and technical subjects had been checked.

Schools no longer have any financial temptation to give prominence to technical, at the expense of humanistic subjects. . . . A number of secondary schools, especially for boys, which used to specialise in their higher forms in science and technology, are extending considerably the teaching of languages, literature and history.

His own particular interest was English, where he noted that the teaching methods were becoming more intelligent, so that, for example, in the study of Shakespeare, more attention was being paid to plot, characterization and style and less to the verbal minutiae. In the same annual report, another inspector, Mr Brereton, described the changes in modern language teaching and the rise of French as a subject to rival Latin. He had a lot to say about the value of the direct method, but noted how hard it was to introduce new methods while still using the old external examinations. 'The remedy,' he wrote, ' . . . seems to lie in the adoption of some system of leaving certificate for senior and junior pupils, respectively, with the examination based on the syllabus of the school itself.' (As it happened, his liberal sentiments were sounder than his prophetic judgement: two years later the Board's Consultative Committee reported on examinations and the result was to reinforce not undermine external examinations by bringing the School Certificate into being.)

There is something uncommonly familiar in the optimistic reports of progress and the hope that the schools might escape from the tyranny of examinations. Every period provides quotations from inspectors – not only in London – who dwell on the liberal changes which they can detect in a few schools where leading spirits are beginning to transform old teaching methods. Other testimony, in the form of memoirs and examination papers, reveals less evidence of progress.

H. M. Burton won a scholarship to Latymer Upper School, Hammersmith, from Langford Road Elementary School, Chelsea, in 1909. Latymer was one of the grant-aided schools to which London sent boys on junior county scholarships. He was to go on up the scholarship ladder to

Cambridge and into a career in teaching and educational administration. In his autobiography* he describes the arid curriculum and the dull and formal teaching methods. If his memory served, the direct method of teaching French had not got very far at Latymer; Latin, science, maths, English and scripture were taught by 'pedantic, unintelligent drudgery', which made no concession to what Mr Brereton would have liked to see.

Burton explains how emphatically the social distinction between the elementary and secondary school was brought home to the secondary school pupil – by the relatively palatial buildings, and by the explanations of the staff who made it clear that those who attended were privileged persons. The secondary schools were seen as great engines of social mobility and the scholarship scheme as a publicly sponsored instrument for elevating clever children from the elementary social classes.

The sociology of a grammar school like Latymer, on which the new maintained secondary schools were modelling themselves, was anything but simple.

Our schoolmasters [wrote Burton] from the headmaster downwards, had nearly all come from the working classes; so had many, if not most of our governors and of the parents. They would probably have admitted if pressed, that sweetness and light were quite as essential as a balance at the bank; they would have accepted in theory the claims of art, of literature and of music, but always they would have added, mentally at least, 'but not for our Cyril!' For them the university scholarship, the double-first, the long years of financially unproductive study, meant a safe, clean job in the end, and the difference it may be, between a maximum of £5 a week as a clerk and £1,000 a year as a headmaster, or a consulting engineer or a chemist. Let the rich look after the arts, they would argue, if subconsciously; our job is to look after security and the material comforts of our children and of their parents.

This was the model which was being reproduced under Morant's code of regulations. But it was still far more obliged to serve a clientele who would leave school at 15 or 16 than the more select few who found their way via the honour board to the university. By 1918, there were still only twenty advanced science courses at the sixth-form level in London secondary schools, only three of them in county schools; only twenty schools in all had advanced courses in modern studies. Only a handful of London schools had advanced courses in the classics.

* *There Was a Young Man* by H. M. Burton.

The same teacher shortage which stimulated the rapid expansion of secondary education and the bringing to an end by the Board of Education's 1904 regulations of the early apprenticeship of pupil teachers, took the Council directly into teacher training. The new authority inherited one important teacher training college – the London Day Training College, which was attached to the University of London, had been opened in October 1902 by the Technical Education Board. Entry to the Day Training College required matriculation, or its equivalent, and was intended for degree students. The higher education committee immediately set about using its powers under the new Act to set up other training colleges for elementary school teachers.

Much of the responsibility for making a success of this – as for the expansion of secondary education – fell on the principal assistant on Robert Blair's staff, Miss Philippa Fawcett, who was appointed in 1905. Her title became assistant education officer for higher education in 1920 till her retirement in 1934.

A legend before she arrived at the L.C.C., Miss Fawcett – daughter of Henry Fawcett, Gladstone's blind Postmaster General, and of Dame Millicent Fawcett, a militant suffragette – had read mathematics at Newnham and been ranked 'above the Senior Wrangler'. At the time of her appointment, she was working in South Africa, helping to establish elementary education in the Transvaal in the aftermath of the Boer War. As Philippa was unable to attend for interview, her mother stood in as proxy.

Having extended its scholarship scheme and included 1,200 probationer scholarships without income limit, aimed at intending teachers between the age of 14 and 16 (£15 for boys, £12 for girls),* the L.C.C. had to make sure there were college places for them to go to. The prevailing view at the time was that school systems should be self-supporting in teachers. London, which was deficient in most kinds of professional and craft-training (as the Llewellyn Smith report had shown fifteen years before), relied upon recruiting large numbers of teachers from the provinces, trained in the voluntary colleges. In 1902, the London School Board appointed 891 new teachers, only 330 of them from colleges situated within the London area.

The first move to redress the balance came with the establishment in 1904 of a training college at Greystoke Place (thirty day students) and the

* The probationer scholarships ran to 16. The scholar then became a pupil teacher for two years before entry to training college.

recognition by the Board of Education of Goldsmiths' College as a college for some 400 students, with ninety-three places set aside for London.

From 1906 the Board of Education stepped up the level of grants for teacher training, and the L.C.C. opened its first residential college for women at Avery Hill Mansion. This became a show-piece, setting a new standard in college buildings and grounds. It was followed by other colleges at Islington, Fulham and Clapham. In 1915, Furzedown College was opened to provide permanent premises for the former Fulham and Clapham colleges. With more extensions at Avery Hill, the total number of college places rose to about 950, which, with the estimated 550 places taken up by future London teachers at the Church colleges, brought the total number of training places in the metropolis up to the number needed if 'subsistence' was to be ensured.

At the same time (1909) some of the colleges were provided with their own demonstration schools. Pope Street School, Woolwich, was attached to Avery Hill. Goldsmiths College took on Clifton Hill, Woolwich. The Fulham Day Training College used Finlay Street, Fulham, while the London Day Training College had Cromer Street, St Pancras. Head teachers in the practising or demonstration schools were treated as members of the college staffs and the assistant teachers were specially selected with training responsibilities in view.

The last pupil-teacher centre in London closed in 1911, and the last pupil teacher gave his last lesson in 1913. George Sampson, a London inspector, aptly summed up the pupil-teacher system in an article for the London Head Teachers' jubilee volume in 1938. 'Taking it in its last and best phase, we may call it a bad system with practical benefits.' So it was: it enabled the schools to operate when their resources were slender; seen in perspective, it was a brilliant device to enable a small number of trained men and women both to control large numbers of pupils and to train their successors. But it made teaching barren and mechanical. Once it became accepted that elementary school teachers should be recruited from the secondary school, the pupil teachers' days were numbered.

An improved supply of teachers was needed to reduce the size of classes as well as to eliminate the uncertificated teachers. In spite of the impressive figures which the London School Board had been able to show for the increase in the teaching force and the reduction in the number of pupils per teacher, classes of over sixty were by no means uncommon. The Board of Education had laid down by regulation that no registered class should exceed sixty. By 1909 the average size of classes in London schools was still as high as forty-five in council schools and thirty-seven in non-provided schools.

These averages concealed some wide variations. One class in seven had more than sixty pupils. Being in flagrant breach of the regulations, London had to negotiate a way out. To encourage a cooperative attitude, the Board of Education began by docking London's grant-in-aid for 1910 by £10,000. To get up to standard, the L.C.C. needed to spend about £5 million and build class rooms for 200,000 children. Agreement was reached on what became known as the '40 and 48' scheme: London promised to go ahead by agreed triennial steps with the reduction of infants' classes to a maximum of forty-eight and senior classes to a maximum of forty. A fifteen-year plan was adopted in 1912. It was interrupted by the war and by successive economic crises after the war. It was not till 1936 that it was finally completed in the council schools, helped more than anything by the decline in the school population and the birth rate fall after the war.

Central schools

One of the pressing questions which the L.C.C. inherited from the School Board was the status and future of the higher elementary schools or higher grade schools whose existence had been threatened by Morant's circular and by the Cockerton judgement. The schools had been allowed to continue on the basis of a competitive entry on the understanding that the pupils had to leave at 15. But the relationship between these schools and the secondary school system and the rest of the elementary system had to be clarified.

One of Blair's assistants, E. M. Rich, sent a report to Blair on the subject in 1905 which Blair annotated and amended before passing on. In the course of it Rich declared:

the proper training for such pupils [i.e. those who wish to stay on] would be ordinary elementary school subjects up to 14, then three years of training in secondary subjects on general humanistic ['humanistic' struck out by Blair] lines, and then a short period of specialisation, technical education ['technical education' struck out] with a view to a future profession ['profession' struck out and 'pursuit' substituted].

Rich's ambitious design seemed to relate more to the third-grade secondary or commercial school expounded by the Taunton Commissioners in 1868 than to the contemporary higher elementary school. The Board of

Education, on the other hand, was determined to limit the higher elementary schools to a more modest role – a three-year course from 12 to 15, firmly linked to the elementary school system, and aimed at preparing boys and girls for employment, yet not pretending to offer specialized trade or commercial training.

The higher elementary schools [wrote an official of the Board, in a letter to the L.C.C. dated 8 August 1907] should not, except as a strictly temporary measure, be used for the education of boys and girls who are intending to become teachers and who will consequently require to continue their education beyond the age limit. . . .

The courses of study must not be framed to lead up to examinations, such as the junior local examinations, which are designed for scholars who will continue their general education to a later age. An external examination should not be taken by scholars in these schools unless that examination is one of a distinctly technical character and is the recognised entrance to employment in some local trade or industry.

A point of dispute between the L.C.C. and the Board concerned the age of entry. The Board wanted 12 to be the minimum. London wanted it to be 11 plus for two reasons: first because many pupils would leave at 14 and the only hope of getting in a three-year course was to let the pupils enter before they were 12. And second, there was the practical reason that selection for the higher elementary schools could then be combined with the junior scholarship examination. (As Blair observed: 'this is very important to a huge system like London'.)

In time the L.C.C. and the Board of Education reached an understanding on the lower age of entry and the L.C.C. was able to go ahead with the development of the higher elementary schools as 'Central Schools', which became the council's policy in 1910. (The old higher grade schools had sometimes been called 'central schools'. They were 'central' in the sense that each served a group of elementary schools.) The *London Education Service* in a felicitous passage defined the central school by stating what it was not. A central school

would not be a trade school because it would train for life as well as livelihood; it would not be simply a primary school because it would train for livelihood as well as life; and finally it would not be a secondary school because of its limited objectives. It would, in short, become neither an inferior secondary school, nor a mere aimless continuation of the primary.

Under the 1910 scheme it was envisaged that London needed sixty central schools of which fifty had been provided by 1914. Half had a commercial bias, nine combined commercial and industrial courses, and the remainder were aimed towards industry. The central schools were, therefore, to become an important part of London's post-primary education with objectives which were clearly defined and strictly limited. They were to be as much conscious of their pupils' future employment as secondary schools were conscious of being preparatory institutions for higher education and professional training.

The arguments which gave rise to the central schools could also be used to support the technical and trade schools which grew in number from the one in 1904 at Shoreditch Technical Institute, where boys learned furniture making, to twenty-one by 1912 (ten for boys, eleven for girls). These schools were reorganized with entry at 13, and became another recognized form of post-primary education for boys and girls who failed to win secondary school scholarships or who, for personal or family reasons, were attracted to vocational courses which more or less guaranteed a craft skill and artisan status.

The technical institutes provided a wide variety of courses: one of the tasks of the first decade was to reduce the rivalry between them and get them to work together to a common strategy. Birkbeck, where degree courses were offered, and Sir John Cass were mainly concerned with evening education. Borough Polytechnic specialized in training technicians and artisans. In others there was day training for apprentices as, for example, for piano-makers at the Northern Polytechnic. The City of London College was concerned almost entirely with commercial education.

When the L.C.C. Education Committee took over from the T.E.B. there were many developments already in hand. The School of Arts and Crafts was completed in Southampton Row. Plans went forward for the Poplar Technical Institute and for the renovation of the Paddington Technical Institute. The Norwood Technical Institute was enlarged and the Hammer-smith School of Arts and Crafts rebuilt. Later (1908) the School of Arts and Crafts became the Central School of Arts and Crafts and a major pioneer in the teaching of industrial design – a 'central' institution in that it was fed by other colleges of art.

The reform of the technical schools and junior departments of the technical institutes was accompanied between 1909 and 1913 by the reorganization of the polytechnics and major technical institutes.

Again it was Rich who worked on this with Blair. Under the scheme introduced in 1913 the junior work was hived off into junior institutes for the 13 plus to 18-year-olds. All the over-18s in the technical institutes were obliged to embark on organized courses requiring at least three evenings' study a week; they were not allowed to take isolated courses only. Most important of all, a number of full- and half-time teachers were appointed to evening institutes as the nucleus of a professional staff.

Close links were formed between the junior commercial institutes and those for senior students, and between the junior technical institutes and the polytechnics and major technical institutes. The accent was placed on the connexion between commercial and technical education and the commercial and industrial firms whose needs had to be met. This was made explicit and effective by setting up advisory committees and seeking to break down the suspicion of practical men and women against which Garnett had fought in the early days of the T.E.B. and from which the technical institutes still suffered.

At the same time as emphasizing this practical and vocational aspect, the new scheme reorganized that part of the further education system which was geared to personal and recreative ends. This included the university extension lectures and the recently started tutorial classes arranged by the Workers' Educational Association – the £150 offered by the L.C.C. to the W.E.A. in 1909 was increased the following year to £300 after H.M.I.s had reported favourably on the courses which were being offered. It also included the much more prosaic activities which some of the evening schools had engaged in, which while offering some general education also provided the opportunity for recreational activities in an educational community.

Some institutes specialized in women's courses, combining these with girls' trade schools; others were devoted to general education. There were institutes for the deaf. And – one of the 1913 innovations – the literary institutes were built up as non-vocational centres offering leisure activities for city-workers. Development of these was cut short by the First World War; nine were re-established in 1919.

Welfare services and special schools

Many of the changes which educational development was bringing were difficult to measure and there were plenty in every generation to question whether more education might not mean worse. But on one topic there was something like unanimity. Writing in *The Times* in March 1924, about the time of his own retirement, Sir Robert Blair observed: 'A great

Midsummer revels at Fulham Central School for Girls, 1932.

Still life: a typical art-room scene from Barnsbury Central School for Boys, 1932.

THINK BEFORE YOU DO FINE THINGS IN A FINE WAY

Craftwork meant carpentry at Shooters Hill School, 1936.

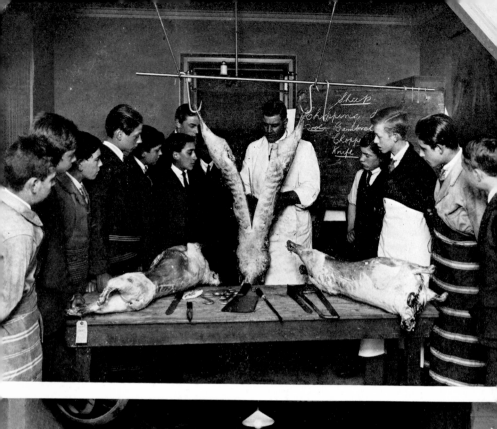

Day continuation schools offered general education and vocational courses on a voluntary day release basis after the short-lived compulsory day continuation schools had closed in 1923.

Retail grocery at Brixton Day Continuation School, 1924.

Top left The butchery class at Battersea Day Continuation School, 1924.

Bottom left A bakery class at the Acland Institute, 1933.

Improving standards in infants' schools included better cloakrooms as at (*above*) Henry Fawcett School, 1937, and brighter, better-ventilated assembly halls as at Coopers Lane, 1936 (*top right*).
Bottom right New furniture and more informal methods at Jessup Road, 1939.

New approaches to language teaching included gramophone records and visual aids – Balham Central School, 1935.

Group music instruction at Catford Central School, 1936.

SCHOOL BUILDING   Old Castle Street School, Whitechapel (*below*), the first
school opened by the London School Board, 1873. At first it was boycotted by
the predominantly Jewish inhabitants of the neighbourhood, till a Jewish head
was appointed.

Top right Thirty years later, the London three-decker style had been
established as, here, at John Ruskin School, Camberwell. *Bottom right*
Thirty years later still, in a more open style, Ealdham Square School gives
each class room access to the playground.

The recreational side of the evening institutes continued to flourish and new subjects were added to the list of courses as, for example, beauty-culture at Barnett Street Evening Institute, 1936.

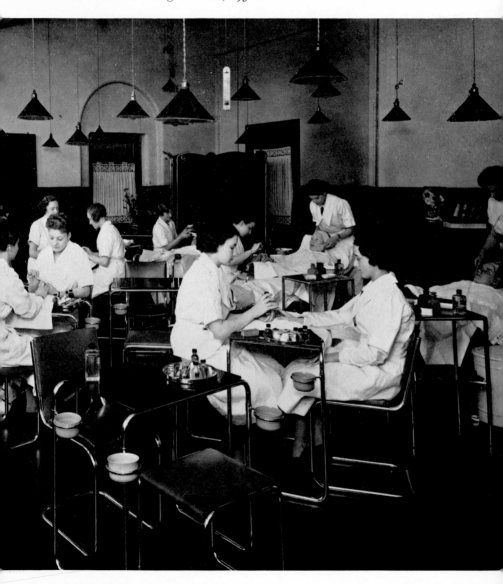

Domestic-science teaching showed the kind of household equipment which girls were expected to use in later life – the laundry class at Carlyle School, 1938.

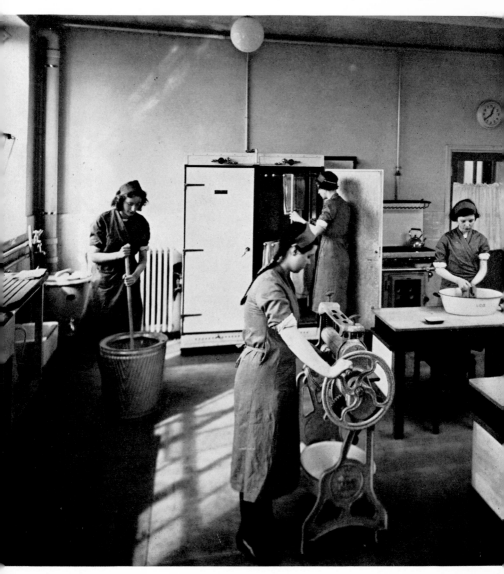

CARE COMMITTEE   Each special school had its care committee of voluntary workers who kept in touch with handcapped children and their homes.

An after-care conference at Durham Hill School, 1937. A girl who is about to leave attends with her mother for advice and assistance.

The care committee workers formed the nucleus of a welfare staff. Here a welfare inspector makes a call in Hoxton, 1939.

WHATEVER YOUR
OCCUPATION

EVENING CLASSES
WILL HELP YOU

WHATEVER YO
HOBBY

Part of an exhibition of students' work at Charing Cross Underground station designed to show the public the range of activities at the evening institutes, 1936.

A cartoon by Grimes used in a big advertising campaign in the summer of 1939, ready for the opening of the autumn term. The outbreak of war put a stop to all evening activity, till in November 1939, improvised classes began to meet in blacked-out premises.

improvement has been effected in the physical character and condition of the children in the elementary schools'. This he attributed to 'greater attention to feeding, to medical (including dental) treatment, to personal cleanliness, to improved methods of physical education, to largely extended facilities for open air games and to the untiring efforts of teachers, doctors, nurses and care committee organisers'.

The first years of the new regime saw a general recognition at the national level that the schools had to be backed up by social and medical services which had yet to be organized. A series of Acts passed by the Liberals at Westminster provided a legal framework for this.

The School Board had employed a medical officer from 1890, and two part-time assistants were appointed in 1898. Most of their work was concerned with the examination of children recommended for special schools or classified as defective, in addition to which they examined pupils who were considered for scholarships and teachers entering the Board's service.

When the Board's medical officer retired in 1902 the post was redefined as a full-time, exclusive appointment as school medical officer at a higher salary – £800 rising to £1,000 – and the first 'ringworm nurses' were appointed to carry out individual and class inspections. Dr James Kerr, the new school medical officer, was an energetic and single-minded campaigner. In his first report to the L.C.C. after the take-over, he dwelt on the appalling conditions in the slum schools. He described in vivid and deliberately savage detail the numerous children with heads 'encrusted with scabs, exudation and lice'. He found ringworm rampant in some schools, with skin diseases such as impetigo and a particularly unpleasant affliction called favus. (In 1906, thirty-three cases of favus were discovered in a small area in Whitechapel and a special school was set up to isolate and treat children suffering from this disease.) The need for a school medical service was clear and during the first three years of the L.C.C. Education Committee era Dr Kerr set about making a start. Britain was still smarting from the discovery that one-third of those who volunteered to join the Army at the time of the South African war were unfit. A committee on 'Physical Deterioration' was set up which led to school medical inspection and school feeding, but the L.C.C. did not wait for the legislation which came in 1907. Cleansing centres were set up in 1904 and in 1905 routine medical inspection was started.

Dr Kerr, according to the historians of the L.C.C.,* was 'able and vigorous but individual in his methods', an oblique way of indicating that

* *History of the London County Council, 1889–1939*, by Sir W. G. Gibbon and R. Bell.

D

he drove ahead with his plans without recognizing any obstacles, bureaucratic or professional. He was confronted with a terrible picture of preventable disease and ill health, malnutrition, and chronic ear, nose and throat conditions and ophthalmia as well as the other ailments and parasitic infestations associated with abominable living conditions and a lack of elementary hygiene.

There were many schools where there were no local hospital facilities for treatment after examination. Dr Kerr, therefore, concentrated his inspections in places where it was possible to arrange treatment. The result was that local hospitals were inundated by demands from parents who would arrive bearing cards issued by the school doctors. This aroused bitter hostility from the hospitals who resented the trouble which the L.C.C. was causing. (In all their dealings with the Council, the hospitals showed extreme touchiness and suspicion lest any working arrangement which they entered into might bring them somehow under L.C.C. control.) It also aroused criticism from the educational side because Dr Kerr's idiosyncratic methods of selecting schools and conducting examinations meant that many schools were left untouched.

The Education (Administrative Provisions) Act, 1907, for the first time placed a duty of medical inspection on local education authorities and also gave them the power to provide treatment as well as examinations. For three years the L.C.C. discussed how these powers should be exercised with the hospitals and with the Board of Education where Dr (later Sir George) Newman was beginning his influential period as Chief Medical Officer.

The prevailing view was that treatment should be provided by the voluntary hospitals or by voluntary committees set up to run treatment centres. Dr Kerr himself opposed this. He did not believe in the voluntary system and wished to set up his own organization. Within the L.C.C., Kerr had to convince the chairman of the Education Committee, Mr Cyril Jackson, and Sir Shirley Murphy, the L.C.C.'s Medical Officer of Health, as well as Blair, and only with their support could he satisfy Sir Robert Morant and Dr Newman at the Board of Education. In the event, the voluntary hospitals won. The Board of Education weighed in with a sweeping attack on the London system. Dr Kerr resigned and the school medical service was brought under the control of the L.C.C.'s new medical officer, Dr William Hamer.

Under the 1907 Act, the Board of Education could require three examinations for each child during the course of the school life. The examinations were more cursory than those which Kerr believed were necessary, but they revealed even more clearly the extent of the need for treatment. Twenty children in every thousand in 1912 were found to be suffering from diseases of the ear; a similar number were found to have impaired hearing.

By the end of 1912 eleven hospitals and seventeen school treatment centres were dealing with 54,000 children in the year. The 1921 Education Act made treatment as well as inspection a duty of the L.E.A. Financial cuts in 1922 brought a set-back to the school medical service, as to much else; instead of depending on full-time doctors, the service had to revert to the pre-1911 system of relying heavily on part-time medical practitioners, to supplement a full-time staff who by 1939 numbered twenty doctors and 420 nurses. There were also seventy-seven part-time dentists, fourteen special advisers and an additional 367 part-time doctors and dentists who helped at treatment centres.

The aim was to provide a preventive medical service, whose success was measured by the reduction in the amount of treatment needed for serious conditions. By the time Gibbon and Bell published their survey of London government in 1939, a great deal had been achieved.

The primary aim of the school medical service is preventive. Only a small part of its time and energy is devoted to providing crutches for lame ducks. Since 1902, when it started, the death rate of children at school age has fallen by more than half; diseases which were rife in the schools have disappeared. . . . Green sickness and severe forms of ophthalmia, such as trachoma, have gone. Blindness, deafness and crippling from tuberculosis have greatly diminished. Of ringworm, which kept more than twenty thousand children away from school in 1901, there are now less than two hundred fresh cases a year in the whole of London; in 1908 when children were first stripped for medical examination, a quarter of them in many districts were found to have verminous bodies; many of the younger school doctors of today have never seen a body louse upon a school child. In 1910 it was possible to find more seriously ill-nourished children in a single school than are now to be found in the whole of London. In 1901 of every hundred children qualified for scholarships ninety-six had to be referred back for severe dental caries and disease of the gums: now the position is almost exactly reversed and the number referred back for dental trouble of the same kind is on average less than four.

In 1906, the Education (Provision of Meals) Act forced the Education Committee to look again at the policy for school feeding. The campaign on behalf of underfed children under the old School Board had continued under the L.C.C., led by representatives of labour organizations and the socialists. For two years after the 1906 Act the L.C.C. continued to rely on voluntary and charitable contributions through a special charitable fund as before. But by 1908 it was becoming clear even to the opponents of free school meals that private benefaction would not suffice: the fund opened by the chairman of the council and the Lord Mayor only raised £12,000. The Education Committee decided to continue to rely as much as possible on voluntary agencies but to offer such help as they could in the form of equipment and some staff assistance.

According to surveys by the School Board's underfed children sub-committee in 1889 and 1899 the number of children coming into the underfed category was about 55,000. At no time did all these receive meals. By the time the L.C.C. Education Committee came on the scene in 1904, it was reckoned that some 27,000 children in 208 schools consumed a weekly average of 66,000 meals. London was doing more than most cities but its 'method, or rather want of method' came in for caustic comment in the report of the Departmental Committee on Medical Inspection and School Feeding in 1905:

> In this as in other matters [the Committee concluded] the vastness of London, its unfortunate lack of a spirit of real local interest, and the ignorance which every Londoner shows of what is going on close to his own door, make effective organization of a proper system of feeding school children a matter of exceeding difficulty.

The meals provided varied from breakfasts of bread and margarine and cocoa to the proverbial 'nourishing soup or stew' which experience showed always went down well. Meals began to be provided more widely still on a mainly self-supporting basis – using the schools' domestic science facilities and cookery centres. In 1905 an experiment began in five cookery centres, allowing the girls to prepare up to fifty dinners at a cost of from $1\frac{1}{2}d.$ to $3d.$ a head. Two years later the experiment was extended where the local managers agreed and the numbers did not fall below eight or the price rise above $3d.$

Finally in 1908–9 the Council decided that more intervention was needed. School meals provided a classic case where public and voluntary social workers had to collaborate or compete. Blair was determined to see that wasteful competition was avoided, while at the same time ensuring that the intervention of public funds did not turn away the voluntary effort. The instrument he devised to replace the Underfed Children sub-committee was the Children's Care sub-committee.

In addition to the central care committee at County Hall, care committees were formed at each school to which the governors were asked to appoint two or three members to serve with 'an equal number of voluntary workers from a list approved by the central care committee', which also nominated another third of the members. A similar organization was set up at the level of the twelve administrative districts into which London was divided. As Blair put it, 'the services of the council's staff of organizers, district organizers and assistant organizers are placed at the disposal of the committees and an endeavour is made to allocate the skilled assistance, especially to those districts where there is most need of workers'.

Blair attached great importance to the development of the care committee and the strategy of public and private collaboration which it represented. He had a deep interest in the school's social function.

Side by side with the increasing attention that is being given to social questions [he wrote] there has been an increased recognition of the importance of the child as an individual organism. The teaching of biological science and psychology have laid stress on the need for treating each child as a distinct individual, with capacities and idiosyncrasies of its own, and have clearly shown how closely related are the physical, mental and moral aspects of child life. These two causes have led to a widening and a deepening of the purpose of education and have placed upon those who administer the educational system the duty of watching over the physical well-being and the general welfare of the children committed to their care.

The care committees became all-purpose instruments. Care committee members checked the circumstances of individual children and decided who should have a free meal. They helped to arrange the medical inspections and ensured that parents took their children to be treated if any illness or defect were discovered. With the heads of schools, they helped to provide the first elements of a vocational guidance and job-finding service and kept in touch with school-leavers in their first jobs. (This was one of their less successful functions. The L.C.C. decided not to exercise powers under the Education (Choice of Employment) Act, 1910, but to continue to work through the juvenile advisory committee set up by the Board of Trade.) They also helped to select children to benefit from the Children's Country Holiday Fund and put necessitous families in touch with other charities like the Shoreditch Boot Committee which could provide clothes and boots. (The Shoreditch Boot Committee raised funds by a public appeal, and then providently went on to organize twice-weekly classes at Mrs Humphrey Ward's play centre in Gopsall Street, where children could learn to cobble and mend their boots when they wore out.)

About 50,000 children were getting free meals by the outbreak of the First World War, the number having dropped to 43,000 in 1913 because, as Blair explained, 'the effect of the Coronation on the labour market' had reduced the number of poor children.

The school meals were usually taken on school premises or at the cookery centres; in many cases the food was sent in ready cooked by a charitable caterer such as the Alexandra Trust. The meals had to be supervised – from the start there was an emphasis on social education and training in good manners – and this, too, was usually a job for care committee members, though in some cases paid supervisors were taken on. The children helped to lay the tables – 'the holding of this office is aspired to by many of the older children, and the training they thus receive should be useful in later life'. The meals sometimes included a 'milk lunch', with biscuit or cod-liver oil usually taken at 11 A.M., said to be 'of great value especially for anaemic children'. (A milk scheme for under-nourished children was inaugurated in 1910, a modest precursor of the more ambitious Milk Marketing Board scheme introduced in 1934 which ensured that, by 1937, about 320,000 were getting free or subsidized milk at school every day.)

The results were quickly noticeable in the rising body weights recorded at the school medical examinations and an increase in muscular strength and activity. In a characteristic comment, Blair reckoned that, even by 1910, a visible change had come to be seen in school athletic and sporting activities.

The children on the necessitous registers, now fully participate in these activities and supply rather above their proportional numbers of prominent performers: this is equally true of swimming. It is indisputable that in the past, lack of nourishment, when it did not entirely exclude, greatly limited the part taken by many children in this, the most attractive side of school life.

(A headmaster added the sour comment that 'I cannot say that the improvement in mentality has been in any way commensurate with the physical improvement'.)

The early years of the L.C.C. Education Committee also saw the consolidation and extension of the work which the School Board had begun with the handicapped and the delinquent. In 1907 the first open-air school was opened at Bostall Wood, Woolwich, to be followed by others after the First World War. By 1929 when the L.C.C. prepared a short book on *The Special Services of Education in London* to explain and expound the system, there were seven day open-air schools for 1,200 children, with two more in the pipeline. There were schools for delicate and anaemic children. As the Medical Officer of Health was quoted as saying, these schools were to meet the needs of a child whose doctor says: 'Now, mother, the thing to do is to get him into the country for a month'.

Within the practice of medicine of the period the schools had an important function – the average duration of a child's stay at an open-air school was eighteen months. Three residential open-air camp schools were also available – the King's Canadian School, Bushey, Barham House, St Leonards, and Wanstead House, Margate. Fresh air, sunlight, good food and regular rest were provided, together with ordinary lessons. Here, as elsewhere, the criterion of success was re-integration into ordinary school or employment at the end.

The first school for children with pulmonary tuberculosis, the Kensal Home School, was set up in 1911, also on open-air lines. Those boys considered fit for vocational training were taught gardening and wood-work. A hostel was set up for girls discharged from L.C.C. homes, with the help of the care committees, and many ex-pupils were successfully found employment. By 1929 the number of TB schools had risen to seven. Most of the children had already spent periods in a sanatorium and continued under the care of the doctors.

As the total school population declined, so too did the numbers in special schools, though the L.C.C. Education Committee's charge was extended in 1930 by the transfer of twenty-three residential schools and homes from the Metropolitan Asylums Board, and with them the respon-sibility for children in care which continued till after the Children Act of 1948. By 1938 there were special school places – day and residential – for some 534 blind, 486 deaf, 2,611 mentally defective and 2,522 physically defective children.

The nursery school movement – though not strictly part of special services for the handicapped – also drew on the same combination of social, medical and educational inspiration. The era of the new authority began at the same time as Margaret McMillan's move from Bradford to London. Having, with her sister Rachel, had a large part to play in making Bradford into an outstanding education authority, Margaret McMillan now

Boys: average height in centimetres

Age	1905	1938	1959
7½	116·0	120·5	123·4
8½	120·5	125·8	129·3
9½	125·2	130·9	134·4
10½	129·8	135·8	139·3
11½	134·3	140·4	144·9
12½	138·7	144·8	149·8
13½	143·1	149·0	155·8
14½	148·3	—	163·2

Girls: average height in centimetres

Age	1905	1938	1959
7½	115·4	119·3	122·4
8½	120·2	124·8	127·7
9½	124·7	130·3	133·2
10½	129·9	135·7	138·7
11½	135·0	141·2	144·5
12½	140·6	146·7	150·2
13½	146·8	152·2	159·2
14½	152·4	—	161·4

Heights and weights of London school children: 1905, 1938 and 1959.

Boys: average weight in kilograms (clothed)

Age	1905	1938	1959
7½	22·02	23·65	24·83
8½	23·47	26·06	28·01
9½	25·46	28·66	30·72
10½	27·59	31·45	33·82
11½	29·95	34·44	37·82
12½	32·46	37·64	41·71
13½	36·40	41·05	46·97
14½	39·23	—	52·91

Girls: average weight in kilograms (clothed)

Age	1905	1938	1959
7½	21·20	22·95	24·49
8½	22·92	25·40	27·22
9½	25·00	28·19	30·56
10½	27·16	31·35	34·03
11½	29·87	34·96	39·00
12½	33·32	39·07	43·84
13½	37·71	43·77	48·99
14½	41·80	—	52·04

began to use her remarkable powers of persuasion and political organization in London in the interest of young children and their physical, emotional and educational development. She pressed for better medical services for the school children and for nursery and open-air schools for the very young, campaigning behind the scenes with politicians and administrators alike, and exploiting her wide circle of influential friends in Government and the L.C.C. In 1914 the L.C.C. opened its first open-air nursery school, the Rachel McMillan school at Deptford.

From 1908 onwards, the Board of Education had recognized that ordinary elementary schools were not ideally suitable for the large numbers of children under 5 in attendance. The 1918 Act included clauses empowering local education authorities to provide nursery schools, but, while the elementary schools continued to receive children below the age of 5, the nursery school movement made slow progress and the medico-social priorities continued to dominate thinking. Great stress was placed at the Rachel McMillan school on the building up of the health of delicate children; the three square school meals a day; the rest period after lunch which is indelibly associated in the popular mind with nursery schools – the rows and rows of children on camp beds having their daily nap.

Within the needs of the time the priorities were right and inescapable. Slowly the need for nursery schools for all children, not just those with poor health or homes, became more widely recognized and the ground was prepared for the 1944 Education Act which gave declaratory support (yet to be carried through) to the idea of a full-scale system of nursery schools below the compulsory school age, as part of the normal service of education.

Juvenile delinquency continued to concern the education authority with responsibility for Industrial schools. Dr Burt prepared surveys exploring the correlations between delinquency and IQ, social background and backwardness. Before the First World War, rising population had made it necessary to extend the list of reformatory and Industrial schools to which London sent boys and girls. More land was bought at Feltham where boys could learn farming. The difficulty of 'disposal' remained; the armed forces, domestic service, the sea, farming (particularly in Wales where the L.C.C. retained an agent) and emigration continued to offer the best prospects.

Juvenile committal proceedings reached new peaks during the early years of the First World War but declined rapidly in the post-war period (partly because of the increased use of probation) and, by the end of the

1920s, declining population helped to reduce still further the numbers being sent to Industrial schools. By 1929 a distinctly optimistic note was being struck in the face of 'the decrease in the amount of juvenile "crime" in London which so fortunately characterises present day conditions'. Better social conditions and better education were seen as mainly responsible for the change for the better. 'Welfare clinics, the school medical service, and other agencies working for better physical conditions have contributed to an improvement which is still noticeably gathering momentum.'

7 *High hopes and low spirits*

After the constructive activity of the first decade of the L.C.C.'s educational era came the war years – the inevitable halt to educational advance followed by the equally inevitable planning for reconstruction in which education figured prominently as a cornerstone of the new Britain.

The schools suffered in predictable ways during the First World War. The number of able-bodied men left in the schools went down at every stage of the conflict and more than half London's 6,000 men teachers joined up. Married women were recalled in large numbers with the retired and the over-age. The total complement of teachers was cut. School visits were curtailed and the museums which were often the object of a visit were closed. Enterprising schools began to take children to the Old Vic instead. The war came into the curriculum inevitably. In his report on the war years, Sir Robert Blair recalled that there was a demand for lesson material on 'how the war came about and why England was right', which was met by pamphlets published by the Oxford University Press. War impinged on the schools even more directly in the form of air-raids. In the worst disaster, in June 1917, an L.C.C. school in Poplar received a direct hit, killing eighteen children. Altogether some fifty tons of bombs dropped on London during the war wrecked ten schools and damaged 239 more.

The medical officers reported, however, that the general health of the children did not suffer. Higher wages of parents in war work bought better food for children in poor areas. The effect on the most measurable kind of poverty was startling: the number of necessitous children, which in the early days of the war had risen from 30,000 to as high as 75,000, had fallen at the close to little over 8,000.

It seems too that, if anything, educational standards rose during the war. The chief examiner for junior county scholarships in 1918 reported his surprise that the percentage of candidates getting high marks had gone up. Further checking showed no technical reason arising from the examination itself why this should have been so. 'The inference', he wrote, 'appears to be irresistible that the increased efforts of teachers and children have triumphed over the obstacles which war had imposed. . . . The work of candidates . . . reveals a decided improvement, which is the more creditable by reason of the difficulties which had to be surmounted.'

London education's most impressive war work was done by the technical institutes and polytechnics which were turned over to producing munitions and precision instruments. This was pushed forward vigorously by Sir Robert Blair who retained a strong personal interest in technical education from his early experience in Scotland and Ireland. Fittingly, the money which the L.C.C. received from the War Department for services rendered at this time was later applied by the L.C.C. to provide scholarships in advanced technology to be known as Robert Blair Fellowships.

A brief boom promised to fulfil the hopes of the 1918 Act. But within four years, slump followed boom and education became a major target for the Geddes axe.

Thereafter the tempo changed and idealism was brought to earth with a bump. Large sections of the 1918 Act became a dead letter and, although the change-over to percentage grants gave the local authorities a fifty per cent, pound for pound, grant from the Exchequer for education, which undoubtedly would have made it harder to hold back development but this was soon modified. Strong leadership from the Board of Education was lacking, and there was the ever-present threat or reality of economic crisis. As Lord Percy of Newcastle (who as Lord Eustace Percy was president of the Board of Education from 1924 to 1929) dubbed it, looking back from the vantage point of the 1950s, it was a period of low spirits.

All the same, education made real if unexciting progress till the Second World War brought evacuation and the dislocation of London's education service. From 1924, when Blair retired, to 1933, George Gater served as London's education officer, his first task being to restore morale in the aftermath of the economy campaign. But he too left on a dying fall, moving on to be clerk to the L.C.C. at the height of the next economic crisis. His successor, E. M. Rich, Blair's old pupil at Aske's and colleague in Ireland and London, was not allowed to escape the same motif of hope and disappointment. The education service rode out the depression as the 1930s progressed; the 1936 Education Act promised to raise the school-leaving age (with certain exemptions) in 1939, only to be overtaken by the chaos of the Second World War.

Even at the height of the depression there was still measurable advance on many fronts, marked by a growing proportion of each age-group in school or full- or part-time education beyond school, and by the continued development of the ancillary services which supported the schools. There was progress, too, in the staffing of the schools, reflected in the achievement of the modest elementary school class-size targets. In the face of inflation and militant campaigning by the teachers, national salaries were established and London, paying the top scale, offered up to £425 a year for men assistant teachers (£340 for women) and up to £650 a year for headmasters and £520 a year for headmistresses. These salaries were cut in 1923 by five per cent and a further five per cent was deducted when the non-contributory pension scheme was put on a contributory basis. Again, in October 1931, teachers' salaries were cut by ten per cent under the National Economy Act, with what in retrospect appear to have been remarkably mild protests from the teachers. They may well have been so relieved that the twenty per cent cut recommended by the May Committee had not been carried into effect that their protests were muted. It was also not without significance that teachers' salaries had been fixed at the height of the post-war inflation when the cost of living index was 140 per cent above the 1914 level; by 1931 it had come down to forty-five per cent above 1914.

The May Committee's other education cuts were commended with a sentence which made their social implications clear:

Since the standard of education, elementary and secondary, that is being given is already in very many cases superior to that which the middle class parent is providing for his own child, we feel that it is time to pause in this policy of expansion, to consolidate the ground gained, to endeavour to reduce the cost of holding it, and to reorganize the existing machine before making a fresh general advance.

The Government's method of carrying out the savings was by cutting the grants to local authorities and issuing a circular (1413) instructing authorities as to what kind of expenditure would be approved for grant. A cut of the order of ten per cent was the aim, though this was not achieved. London cut its education budget by £1.5 million, but the Exchequer grants were reduced by £1.7 million and rates had to rise accordingly.

In London, as elsewhere, every item in the education budget was scoured. Some £39,000 was to be saved by changing the scholarship and maintenance regulations for secondary schools, which involved a cut in grant for existing scholarship-holders as well as future scholars. Higher fees raised £30,000. Some £2,500 was saved by shortening the midday break, thus reducing the hours schools had to be heated and lighted. Caretakers took a 2½-5 per cent pay cut. School prizes were abandoned with a consequent saving of £12,500. (This was pilloried in the press and elsewhere as the last word in meanness, and helped Labour to win the 1934 London election.) Capitation allowances were held down. Replacement of old furniture was postponed. Painting and decorating was rephased. Plans for setting up new care committees were put off. Two new special schools at Downham and Bellingham were temporarily dropped. Governors of schools were all asked to suggest their own savings: the first fifty-one suggestions yielded savings of £40,000.

By 1934 it was already possible to start restoring the cuts – making a grant of £12,500 to London University, bringing down the income limits for junior county scholarships, preparing a new triennial development programme and pressing on with reorganization.

The scars remained. A change of party leadership helped to underline the traumatic effect. But the impact of the economic crisis on the schools was less in reality than in the legend which formed around it. To some extent the blow was cushioned because elementary school rolls were falling – when staff numbers were going down yet staffing ratios were improving. This like the decline in living costs is so unlike more recent experience that it takes an effort of the imagination to appreciate the dulling effect which it had, as the average age of London teaching staff crept up. With falling rolls, staff complements were reduced and it was not uncommon for teachers to have to leave the schools they served and move to other vacancies if no one else happened to be retiring or leaving for other reasons.

In another respect, however, the schools benefited. In London, as in other areas, the secondary schools were able to select first-class graduate recruits at a time when there were unemployed graduates looking for jobs. For the next forty years, the schools would continue to benefit by the numbers of excellently qualified science and arts graduates who joined the teaching staff during the depression.

8 Reconstruction

In 1916, H. A. L. Fisher moved from the office of vice-chancellor at the University of Sheffield to become President of the Board of Education in succession to Mr Arthur Henderson. Before he arrived, the need for post-war educational reform had already been noted and a departmental committee under the chairmanship of J. Herbert Lewis, M.P., Parliamentary Secretary to the Board, had been set up to study 'juvenile education in relation to employment after the war'.

The Committee examined the census figures and the Board of Education statistics and produced a table showing just how small a section of the teenage community was being touched by public education immediately before the First World War.

	Children and young persons aged between					
	12–13	13–14	14–15	15–16	16–17	17–18
Percentage in full-time course	91	66	12	4	2	1
Percentage in part-time course	4	9	16	14	13	10
Percentage unenrolled	5	25	72	82	85	89

Private education was not included, which meant that about five per cent at most could be deducted from the unenrolled figures.

'Practically . . . ,' concluded the Committee, 'public education after the elementary school leaving age is a part-time affair. And there is very little of it.'*

* For an echo nearly fifty years later, see the opening paragraphs of the Crowther Report, 1959: 'this report is about the education of English boys and girls aged from 15 to 18. Most of them are not being educated. . . . '

The policy put forward by the Lewis Committee took legal form in the 1918 Act. The leaving age was to be 14 without any exceptions. And boys and girls who left at 14 or 15 were to be required to continue in part-time education for not less than eight hours a week or 320 hours a year.

The Lewis Committee were much impressed by the upheaval caused by industrial mobilization – the disruption of juvenile industrial training and the continued use of young workers of under 14 under the rules for part-time exemptions. One of the reports which influenced their thinking was an investigation of *Boy Labour* by Mr Cyril Jackson, a former chairman of the L.C.C. Education Committee.

In the middle of 1916, Blair had introduced a memorandum on educational reconstruction and set up a series of conferences to consider the several ages and stages of the education service. He acknowledged the healthy discontent with the educational system which the war had aroused, relating this to the tendency, 'after all great wars, in fact after all great upheavals of civilization', to fall back on '"the best possible education" as an insurance for the future, both of the individual and of the state'.

While clearly regarding this reforming zeal with a certain scepticism, he felt that 'we ought to take advantage of the existing state of public feeling and to draw from it as much energy as we can for the improvement of our educational system'.

Having noted the haphazard way in which the English educational system had grown, and how this haphazard quality had been elevated to the status of a valuable tradition as the antithesis of dull and rigid uniformity, he insisted that 'our pride in the great revolutions effected by the Acts of 1870 and 1902 need not blind us against the need for further improvement. . . . What we want is, I think, progress without breach of continuity.'

He began by sending a chit round his senior staff. He asked a single question: 'If you were an autocrat, and had the means of carrying out your will, what are the six reforms in education which you would carry out and the order in which you would do them? Only heads are wanted; no reasons need be given. Monday morning will do for reply.'

The replies he received are interesting because they give some indication of the ideas which were being mooted at the time when Fisher was planning the 1918 Act, and its abortive predecessor.

An inspector, I. H. Jones, put forward a shopping list which probably accorded closely to the consensus position:

1. To place within the reach of every child a bright, attractive, well-planned and suitably equipped school building with a commodious playground.
2. To reduce the size of classes.
3. To raise the leaving age of elementary school children to 16, with compulsory attendance at continuation schools till 18.
4. To make the teacher's position as regards training, emoluments, prospects and conditions of work such as would make the teaching profession more attractive.
5. The further development of scientific and technical education and the abolition of antiquated systems of weights and measures and non-decimal coinage.
6. Abolition of the half-time system in manufacturing areas.

Mr Brereton also stressed the raising of the leaving age to 16; he wanted bigger education areas (Greater London), a closer assimilation of central schools to secondary schools, with a reciprocal influence on each, and increased craft training in schools providing 'more essential preparation for livelihood'.

Dr Cyril Burt selected, as might have been expected, priorities connected with the measurement of educational abilities:

1. Census of educational abilities of the school population periodically repeated and entailing:
   (a) estimates of educational facilities required by different degrees and kinds of ability;
   (b) standards of achievement, optimal as well as minimal, attainable under different conditions and at crucial stages in the school career;
   (c) tests of progress or deterioration in the educational system or its branches;
   (d) allocation (as far as possible) of individuals of appropriate ability to appropriate vocations.
2. Research centres:
   (a) for the testing of methods of teaching;
   (b) for studying exceptional individuals, super-normal as well as sub-normal.
3. Residential School Communities for those whose home conditions and parental treatment are inadequate to their abilities and disabilities.
4. A revised curriculum, no longer tending to ignore:
   (a) the training of 'reasoning' in favour of suggestibility;
   (b) the training of 'emotions' (i.e. the instinctive moral and aesthetic sources of character);
   (c) the child's material and social environment as it appeals to him;
   (d) the child's future status as a citizen and as a worker of a specific class.
5. Cautious application of the more plausible methods of so-called 'scientific business management', to the administrative work of teachers and minor officials.

6. An attempt to create a scientific profession of teaching by:
   (a) modifying methods of training, appointment and promotion;
   (b) multiplying facilities for observation and research;
   (c) collecting and publishing reports on educational problems, based upon exact records, experiments and statistics, not merely upon conferences and discussions;
   (d) ... teachers' associations to become scientific bodies rather than debating societies or trade unions.

Day continuation schools was a recurring theme, showing the prevailing apprehension about the state of industry after the war and the vivid memories of labour troubles in the immediate pre-war period.

A series of memoranda emerged from Blair's conferences. That on elementary education stressed the differing conditions in different parts of the metropolis; under Cyril Burt's probing eye, differential standards of performance and ability were being more systematically checked and charted, and there was a reference to taking steps to ensure that special care for the super-normal child should become a recognized need like care for the backward.

Another theme was the relationship between the schools and industry and commerce. Familiar criticisms were carefully rehearsed: businessmen were said to complain of insufficient attention to 'the essentials of elementary education', and a lack of initiative among the boys and girls.

In one of his memoranda, Blair speculated on what was to become the Hadow formula for the restructuring of elementary education so that there was a break at 11: up to 11 children would attend an infants' and junior school, to be followed by a senior school from 11 to 14 plus. The conference on the future of secondary education was urged to bear the needs of central schools in mind. 'The secondary school conference,' Blair insisted, 'should direct its attention particularly to the relationship of the central school to the secondary school.'

A selection system in which the first creaming went to the grammar school and the second to the central school, highlighted the anomalous position of the fee-payers, who at this time formed a high proportion of the grammar schools' early leavers. Many of the fee-payers were less intelligent and less able to cope with the secondary school programme than many who were sent to the central school. Yet the central school was pegged resolutely to its limited objectives, while the grammar school was equally firmly geared to aims which were inappropriate to perhaps a quarter of its population. (Also, the cost to the rate-payer of subsidizing the *fee-payer's* secondary schooling was more than the whole cost of a central school place.)

The 1918 Act followed closely the lines along which London had been thinking, including the fifty per cent grants which benefited London particularly. (It was reckoned that in London in 1914, seventy-three per cent of the cost of education was being met from the rates, while in the rest of England and Wales the percentage was only fifty-three.)

By 1920, when the L.C.C. produced a draft scheme under the 1918 Act – a document running to some 112 pages – the authority could boast (not without a manifest self-satisfaction) that 'many of the developments foreshadowed by the Act . . . had already been anticipated by the London authority'. The scheme provided for an increase in the number of secondary school places from 18,315 to 21,000 (for boys) and from 18,772 to 20,217 for girls. The figures fell short by about 1,500 and 2,300 respectively of the estimate of one place per hundred of the population laid down by the Board of Education, but the nineteen projects proposed in the scheme were put forward as the minimum programme to be achieved without delay and capable of being increased later.

Considerable controversy surrounded the L.C.C. policy over scholarships and maintenance grants. The law left a great deal to the discretion of the authority: the council had a duty to ensure that secondary education was available for all who were capable of profiting by it. But what test of 'capacity to profit' to use, what income scale to apply, and how to select recipients for grants, were all questions for debate. The L.C.C. rejected the idea of grants for all poor students – as indeed the House of Commons had done – and decided to continue to set their own competitive examination even if this meant excluding some pupils from the elementary schools who were more 'capable of profiting' in the grammar schools than many of those admitted as fee-payers. The position was fraught with ambiguity and illogicality but the council rejected any attempt to raise the admission standards for fee-payers in county secondary schools because this would divide some schools into two classes, 'to one of which admission would be based on social status, rather than on intellectual attainment'. The detailed proposals provided that the authority should continue to offer 1,600 L.C.C. scholarships to secondary schools at 11 plus each year and 5,000 places in central schools, to be followed at 13 by 300 supplementary junior scholarships and 150 bursaries for intending teachers. Pupils remaining beyond 16 and 17 plus were expected to take the first school examination; to be considered for a university scholarship they had to take the second school examination at 18 or 19 plus.

The upper income limit for free places was set at £450 a year (after certain deductions) for the 11- and 13-year-old entrants. Beyond that it was raised to £550 a year; for university awards it was £750 a year.

There was little left of the radical ideas which had been circulating a few years earlier, and the secondary scheme was still a series of obstacles for clever ex-elementary pupils to clamber over, while the middle-class children were expected to go through secondary education as of right. As Dr Haden Guest, an L.C.C. member who later became a Labour M.P., put it in *The New Education*, a critique of the London Plan published in 1920, 'the whole idea of publicly provided education is, up to the present, too much dominated by the conception which is expressed in the phrase "children of the elementary school type". As the scheme itself shows, this conception is out of date and has in practice to be discarded.'*

'More and more,' wrote Haden Guest, 'the problem simply is one of providing the citizens of London as a whole with the education they require, irrespective of class and irrespective of financial position.' He advocated saving money on bricks and mortar – deliberately building schools to last not more than thirty years or so – instead of continuing the solid tradition of the old London three-deckers.

As for the central schools which were part of London's compromise answer to the need for more secondary school places, London had fifty-one such schools by 1920 and planned to raise this number to 100. But this was undermined by a report by H. E. Haward, financial comptroller to the L.C.C., in which he urged caution. He noted that the L.C.C. had not yet carried out its earlier programme of sixty central schools and urged that

the proposals should be limited for the present to the provision of a smaller number of places and the position reviewed when it is seen to what extent the pupils in central schools avail themselves of the fifth year of the course, as it

* Dr Guest might have noticed an unconscious progression in the use of the phrase 'elementary school type' from the older and more familiar 'elementary school class'. The system was, of course, still consciously class-based. But liberal-minded educationists tended to seek a way out of the class basis of secondary education by substituting a different scheme based on 'types'. As it happened, the types bore a striking correlation to the earlier classes, but, conceptually, the idea marked a new stage in the development of ideas on secondary education. Thus in his seminal pleas for secondary education for all, Tawney held up as an objective that 'all normal children, irrespective of the income, class or occupation of their parents, may be transferred at the age of 11 plus from the primary or preparatory school to *one type or another* of secondary school and remain in the latter till 16'.

might conceivably transpire that a large proportion of the pupils would prefer to leave the central schools . . . to become wage-earners and go to day continuation schools.

The most important development outlined in the 1920 scheme was the plan for twenty-two compulsory day continuation schools, the first of which were to open in January 1921. Pupils were to attend eight hours a week in two sessions of four hours each, for a course of general education from 14 to 16. Under the plan, the requirement was to be extended to the 16–18 age group in 1928, for whom courses with a vocational bias would be provided. Each school was to have 360 places and be open from forty-four to forty-eight weeks a year. A rapid build-up of 15,000 students a quarter was planned to a total of 120,000. Some 800 instructors were to be appointed the first year and another 800 the second year and the initial cost worked out at £247,500 rising to £1 million.

The scheme went ahead as planned and in January 1921 the first batch of day continuation schools were operating in old school buildings and hired premises. Improvisation on the grand scale by the head teachers and their staffs overcame the early difficulties and the schools settled down to establish their own curricula and build up working relationships with employers, on whose goodwill they depended in practice.

From the first there were major obstacles in the way, caused by the failure of other local authorities in the London region to enforce the day continuation clauses of the 1918 Act. Employers compared the position in London with that outside: compulsory day release in London amounted to a form of tax on juvenile labour which was not levied across the border in neighbouring counties and boroughs. At a time of rising unemployment this point was readily seized on in discussion. Industrialists objected to what they regarded as discrimination against them: parents feared that, in some way, the day continuation legislation might make it more difficult for their sons and daughters to get scarce juvenile jobs.

Nevertheless, by February 1922, the L.C.C. Higher Education Committee received an enthusiastic report on the first year's work, full of optimism about the future. By now the number of schools had built up to thirty-five, housed in ninety-five buildings, fifty-nine of them hired by the L.C.C. to augment the school buildings which were available. Some 47,000 students were enrolled. Early prejudices were in the process of being dispelled and the main conclusion seemed to be that the value of day continuation schooling was so great that it was going to be important to extend the age range upwards as soon as possible, to cover more and more of the 14–18 age group.

But unemployment was rising and the slump brought its associated crisis in public finance. When the Government announced a programme of economy measures, which included the decision not to enforce the day continuation sections of the 1918 Act, the L.C.C. Education Committee had to reconsider their quixotic position as (with a handful of others) lonely progressive models to the rest of the country. Being an enclave of day-release surrounded by less enlightened neighbours was possible for a while in the expectation that the rest would soon follow London's example. Without Government backing and a clear intention to press ahead with the policy nationally, London (unlike Rugby) was in no position to go it alone.

In June 1922, having sent a deputation to discuss the matter with Mr H. A. L. Fisher, the L.C.C. Education Committee decided not to reopen the schools after the summer holiday. With Fisher's encouragement, they substituted a more modest scheme for ten day continuation colleges on a voluntary basis in the attempt to salvage something from the wreck. The estimated expense was £80,000 a year – a third of the initial cost of the larger programme – and schools were retained in the City and at Westminster, Islington, Greenwich and Woolwich, Battersea, Homerton, Brixton, Hammersmith and Southwark and Bermondsey. Pupils were to be admitted on day release; they could also attend up to half-time if they were still awaiting employment. The build-up of numbers was slow but encouraging: 4,071 for the autumn of 1922, followed by 4,678 and 4,941 for the first two terms of 1923.

It was also at this time (the winter of 1923), when juvenile unemployment was mounting to new heights, that the L.C.C. began to organize instructional and recreational centres for unemployed youths of 16 to 18 at the request of the Ministry of Labour, which paid three-quarters of the cost. Up to 3,700 youngsters attended. As the spring and summer drew on, numbers declined and only four centres were kept open.

The centres were staffed largely by teachers, though not without difficulty because, through bureaucratic rigidity, teachers who worked in them were not eligible for superannuation benefits.

9 *Secondary education for all*

As the story of London education unfolds and becomes more diffuse during the 1920s and 1930s, one theme stands out. The concept of elementary education as a self-contained, class-based system of schools, alongside a secondary and preparatory system, was becoming increasingly impossible to sustain. The answer in 1944 was to divide the schools into primary and secondary stages, in a serial instead of parallel relationship. This was summed up in the idea of 'secondary education for all', a slogan which conveniently meant different things to different people.

Before change could come, there had to be repeated demonstrations of the social and educational limitations of the divided system. To describe how this took place in London would be a study in itself. All that can be done here is to spotlight a few episodes on the way, starting with a survey of London secondary schools carried out by a young sociologist in 1923–4, and going on to look at the reappraisal carried out by the Labour Party on gaining control of the L.C.C. in 1934, the survey of senior schools undertaken by the L.C.C. inspectorate in 1939, and the drawing together of all these different strands in the preparation of the London school plan between 1944 and 1947.

Social progress and educational waste

This was the title of a book published in 1926 by Kenneth Lindsay, a research worker who carried out a sociological study of secondary schools in London and a number of other provincial cities and counties under the guidance of R. H. Tawney, the economic historian. While writing the book in 1923–4, Lindsay – an old boy of St Olave's Grammar School, Bermondsey – had held a fellowship at Toynbee Hall. Later he was to enter Parliament and, as Independent National M.P. for Kilmarnock Burghs, served as a Parliamentary Secretary at the Board of Education in the immediate pre-war years.

Lindsay found that in England and Wales as a whole, 9·5 per cent of the elementary school-leavers went on to the secondary schools – and that of these one-third had free places and two-thirds paid fees. One per thousand went on to the university.

Against this national average, Lindsay showed that in London only 6·4 per cent went on to grammar schools; this in the metropolis which had consistently boasted of its high standards. Elsewhere, some twenty-seven per cent transferred to grammar schools in pace-setting Bradford which, like Manchester, Salford and Sheffield, had abolished fees in maintained secondary schools.

Looking back to this period from thirty years later, Lord Eustace Percy judged that it was at this time that 'the demand for real "equality of opportunity" was becoming nothing less than the main popular motive for political action'. It was, he said, far more clearly recognized at the local than the national level. Surveys like Lindsay's showed why. Not only was London less than averagely well equipped with grammar schools: access to grammar schools varied enormously from one part of London to another. Lindsay examined the 1919 scholarship record in seven 'poor' London areas – Bethnal Green, Lambeth, Limehouse, Poplar, Shoreditch, Battersea North and Paddington North – and found that they won 125 junior county scholarships – an average of 1·3 scholarships per 1,000 pupils. He compared this with the record for seven 'rich' London areas, Brixton, Dulwich, Hampstead, Lewisham, Streatham, Kensington South and Woolwich, where some 245 children won scholarships, 5·3 per 1,000 of the elementary school population. The average for London as a whole was 2·6 per 1,000.

Even within areas a few elementary schools succeeded in carrying off a disproportionate number of scholarships: in Bermondsey, Keetons Road and Alma schools, situated in the 'best' neighbourhood, won 112 out of 309 scholarships gained in Bermondsey between 1914 and 1923. There were individual schools in Lewisham, like Stillness Road, which won more scholarships than all the elementary schools in Bermondsey.

Piling on the evidence, Lindsay showed that whereas Dr Cyril Burt, the L.C.C. psychologist, had estimated that ten per cent of children in London schools were 'backward' – that is, unable to do the work of the class one

Figures indicative of the relation between impoverished environment and the educational attainments of London children:

| | Number of schools: 1919 | | | per 1,000 |
	B	G	Total	
Seven poor areas				
Bethnal Green	11	14	25	1·2
Lambeth	1	4	5	0·5
Limehouse	10	8	18	1·3
Poplar	7	12	19	1·5
Shoreditch	11	6	17	1·0
Battersea North	8	21	29	2·3
Paddington North	2	10	12	1·8
	50	75	125	1·3 average
Seven better areas				
Brixton	1	15	22	3·4
Dulwich	20	20	40	6·3
Hampstead	9	14	23	4·3
Lewisham	39	33	72	7·7
Streatham	17	8	25	5·8
Kensington South	7	8	15	5·1
Woolwich	30	18	48	5·0
	129	116	245	5·3 average
London as a whole	789	779	1,568	2·6

year below that normal for their age – the proportion of backward children was as high as twenty per cent in Lambeth and as low as one per cent in Lewisham.

Bradford provided the shining example. There a much more modest standard was required in the qualifying examination and nearly sixty per cent qualified. But even so, more than half of those qualified turned down the grammar school place although no fees were charged.

London [wrote Lindsay] has chosen another way out of the difficulty if indeed it should not be described as an evasion of it. Although the total population of maintained secondary schools has doubled in the last ten years, the percentage of free places to fee payers has actually diminished. An alternative in the shape of 60 central schools has been provided and each year some 5,000 children are drafted in to these schools.

The analysis of social class corresponded to the imbalance suggested by the geographical survey. Only 3·2 per cent of the grammar school entrants were the children of unskilled workers. Only ten per cent of grammar school leavers went into industrial employment. In Bradford, on the other hand, some seven per cent were the children of unskilled workers and twenty-one per cent went into industrial occupations.

On Lindsay's analysis, some forty per cent of the fathers of grammar school pupils were skilled workers, thirty-five per cent came from the official and clerical classes, ten per cent were shop-keepers. The rest of the pupils, about fifteen per cent, were made up of the children of widows (ten per cent plus) and unskilled workers.

There were disproportionately many children whose parents were in the building trades and few who were engaged in transporting Londoners and their goods. The garment industry with a high Jewish minority was well represented. The most obviously under-represented group was the dockers and the general labourers who were virtually untouched by the scholarship system.

This was presented against the background of rising juvenile unemployment: fifteen per cent of 14–16-year-olds in Bermondsey were out of work. It had been reckoned that as many as forty per cent of those 14-year-olds who did get jobs became errand boys with nothing to look forward to except unemployment later on. Some 6,500 juveniles were registered as out of work, but this was regarded as an underestimate.

In probing the social class basis of the new secondary education, Lindsay was influenced by Tawney and in turn helped to feed the Labour minority in the L.C.C. with new ammunition. Lindsay's own remedy was greatly to increase the number of grammar school places and also to extend the central schools on the basis that fifty per cent of the age group could profit by post-primary education to 16. His book appeared in 1926. So did the Hadow Report on the *Education of the Adolescent* (which also owed a great deal to Tawney who was a prominent member of the Consultative Committee which produced it) which fathered the reorganization of primary and secondary education into separate, successive stages. Two years earlier, in 1924, London had begun its own reorganization into junior and senior elementary schools with a break at 11, as outlined in the Blair memorandum referred to earlier.

Critical view from Labour, 1934-5

In the 1934 elections, the Labour Party displaced the Municipal Reform group as the majority party of the L.C.C. Within days of taking control the Labour Party had begun to advertise the presence of a new regime. Empire Day, traditionally celebrated with enthusiasm in London schools, was changed to Commonwealth Day. The General Purposes Sub-Committee resolved in favour of raising the school-leaving age to 15. Technically it was possible to do this by making a bye-law but it was plain that there would be chaos if London went ahead alone without the surrounding areas (as had happened with the day continuation schools), and the Government was urged to nominate 1 April 1935 as the appointed day for the whole country. Estimated cost for London: £750,000 a year and a capital sum of £135,000 – no more than had recently been spent on a single polytechnic. The cost of extra maintenance allowances had been estimated at £288,000.

There were echoes here, of course, of the crisis which had brought down the second Labour Government in 1931. With high unemployment, raising the school-leaving age took on a different aspect as social relief. Sir John Gilbert, the former chairman, now leading in opposition, condemned the proposed use of education money as 'a palliative for social ills'. Significantly, the raising of the leaving age was a universal topic of speculation in educational circles. Falling school rolls held out promise of enough school places by the end of the decade.

Next, under the influence of Hugh Franklin, Mrs Helen Bentwich's brother, the new Education Committee set up a joint sub-committee of the Elementary and Higher Education Committees to examine post-primary education of all kinds.

Rich, who by now had succeeded Gater, put up a committee paper which was defensive in tone. He showed how the London elementary school roll had decreased from 1914 (727,000) to 579,000 in 1932-3, and how it was expected to decline to 450,000 by 1939-40. Secondary, technical and central school places, however, had risen from 61,305 in 1920 to 83,560 in 1933–4 as follows:

	1920	1925	1930	1933–4
Central	17,000	22,000	28,500	31,740
Secondary	41,416	42,666	46,050	45,780
Junior technical	2,889	3,787	5,418	6,040
	61,305	68,453	79,968	83,560

Thus opportunity had expanded fairly rapidly, particularly in the central and technical schools, and there were some 2,000 places in the various types of specialist post-primary school which were now unfilled.

In addition, Rich could now point to the progress of Hadow reorganization: about 100,000 pupils were now in reorganized senior schools. He defended the central schools for the distinctive contribution they made 'as an essential part of the educational system' performing different functions from those of the grammar schools.

Justifying the scale of London's provision, Rich estimated the annual entry as follows:

	Entrants	Percentage of age groups
Central	8,610	15·7
Secondary	8,500	15·4
Junior technical	2,040	3·7
	19,150	34·8

These figures compared favourably with other areas operating similar schemes, though few had London's proportion of junior technical schools – a quarter of all the technical schools in England and Wales were in London.

In a concluding section, he stressed the high standard of London's central and technical schools and the need to make sure that there were suitable employment opportunities available if post-primary education was to be expanded. Because of the declining population, London's eighty-seven central schools provided the same proportion of places as the 1920 scheme for 100 central schools had proposed, and the standard of grammar school provision was about three per cent better than the one place per 1,000 of population put forward in 1920.

Everything possible [Rich added] should be done to educate the public to the view that all three types are of equal importance and offer equal, if different, advantages; and that every pupil ought, in his own interests, to go to the type which is most suitable . . . for his future life and employment. . . . Better facilities for transfer . . . are essential. . . . It is not easy, for apart from the reluctance of schools to part with pupils, there are inherent disadvantages in moving from one school to another.

Meetings were held throughout the winter of 1934–5. Rich continued to urge the merits of the scheme which had already been established 'to provide suitable opportunities for all children with the ability to profit by the various courses of education'.

The great majority of London's children are destined to pursue occupations which will make little demand upon specialised gifts. . . . To give a more expensive form of education, therefore, to more than a proportion of London children would be misuse of the educational system. . . . It is . . . advisable . . . to concentrate expensive forms of educational training in relatively few schools, in which efficiency is ensured by the homogeneity of the pupils and of their purpose. Anything which would lower the standard of such schools would be most regrettable. It is questionable whether, even at present, we do not admit to them, too freely, children of mediocre gifts. It is characteristic of the British character that the spirit of healthy competition should provide the necessary stimulus to effort. This finds expression in our scholarship system . . . in such a way that children even at an early age shall strive for facilities denied to the idle or indifferent. It is equally important that those of less capacity should become aware of their own limitations, both as a spur to effort, and as an understanding of the conditions in which they are likely to enter adult life and the part they are likely to play in the life of the country.

The Joint Committee took a less rosy view, without being able to suggest much which could be done. It had little difficulty in pointing out the weakness of early selection at 11 plus: 'even where children at such an early age show signs of particular bias or aptitude it is doubtful whether this will be their bias and aptitude in adolescence, while the very act of grading in separate scholastic strata produces an inevitable consciousness of difference which is harmful to the development of character'.

The Sub-Committee was unimpressed, but the legal and financial complications attending any radical change were too great for London alone. On this, their advisers were adamant. Legislation was required if the various strands of post-primary education were to be drawn together – as it was, the four types of school were administered under three different sets of regulations, and in many areas by more than one authority. Parts of the report, however, were not without prophetic interest: it referred to

the desirability of establishing a system of post-primary education which will function as an integral whole rather than in separate departments or types of school like the present system. . . . We have considered a suggestion that this unity of post-primary education might be achieved by the *establishment of a new type of school* which would be large enough to provide within its four walls most, or all, of the activities now carried on in existing types of post-primary school. Some exceptions for special arrangements with technical establishments, would probably have to be made for providing the instruction now so success-fully given in Junior Technical Schools. . . . The new type of schools would be organised in such a way that a good general education could be given for the first few years of the course, during which the pupils would find their proper level and bent through the adoption of the 'sets' system; thereafter, special facilities would be available for differentiations in the curriculum according to the abilities and aptitudes of the pupils. In such a 'multi-type' or 'multi-bias' school, it should be comparatively easy to transfer a pupil from one side to another according to the development of his interests and abilities, without incurring any psychological disturbances such as may arise from a further change in the locale of his school. . . . We are of the opinion that more fluidity between all types of post-primary school is desirable, in order to secure that every pupil gets the type of education most suitable to his ability and particular bent. We think that the 'multi-type' school offers a means of achieving this.

. . . Entry to the school would be automatic without any special competitive examination. Besides overcoming the difficulties of fluidity already referred to, the 'multi-type' school would get rid of the disparities which now exist in the cost, equipment and general administration of the various types of post-primary schools. It would also help to break down any prejudices which may exist regarding the relative merits of one type of post-primary education as compared with another.

Senior schools, 1939

As the third decade drew to an end a full report on the senior schools was called for from the London inspectors. It was a suitable time to carry out an audit. The school-leaving age under the 1936 Act was due to be raised in September 1939 – the inspectors' report appeared in April. Of 532 council elementary schools, some 477 had been reorganized on an 11 plus basis; thirty more schemes were in hand, leaving only twenty-five unreorganized schools without new arrangements. Progress among the non-provided schools was slower. Only ninety-three out of 352 had been reorganized, but some 204 schemes were in hand with the assistance of the 1936 Act, and most would be dealt with 'in the next few years'.

Again the tone was defensive. Declining numbers meant that staff were ageing and new teachers with energetic new ideas tended to be at a discount. There were schools where the PE equipment could not be used because there was no one young and agile enough to supervise its use. Pupil numbers had dropped by twenty-five per cent in nine years since 1930.

The inspectors concluded that lower standards were to be expected as the percentage drawn off to selective schools increased. Dr Cyril Burt had calculated that only about fifty per cent of the elementary school children in 1915 were in standard VI or better. By 1939, with a high degree of creaming to other schools, it was estimated that only a third of the children reached the equivalent of a standard VII, a third reached standard VI and a third reached standard V or below. A sixth of the children – about sixteen per cent – were judged to be backward.

The disorganization associated with 11 plus reorganization was blamed for some of the schools' difficulties:

it should be recorded that many unavoidable circumstances have combined to produce working conditions distinctly unfavourable to the progress of the junior-senior type of school reorganization in its early years. It is scarcely to be expected that an extensive advance could have been made during such a period.

As for the curriculum and content, the tone is not unlike that of the Newsom Report some twenty-four years later, except that it is more tentative and can give less specific examples of the liberal practice which it desires to encourage.

'Nearly all' senior schools were judged to have made some kind of valuable contribution. Relations between pupils and teachers were changing and becoming easier, schools were happier, cooperative endeavour was greater. As in all previous reports on elementary school curricula there was approval for school visits and for craft and practical work. But, said the inspectors, in important respects the task of these schools had barely begun: 'in the treatment of subjects such as history, geography and science and even in the basic skills, they are still somewhat uncertain and often ineffective'.

Some of the blame was passed on to the junior schools: many of the children had low attainment in reading which was blamed in part on background. But the junior schools were also blamed for setting too hot a pace, spurred on by the 11 plus, and also, amid the compliments for the infants' school and activity methods, there were the ever-present doubts about the demands new methods placed on teachers with large classes. Even so, 'consideration of the best infant schools which apply modern methods shows that ability to read appropriate matter by the age of about 7 plus is a reasonable expectation for most children'. If the school-leaving age were to be raised, they forecast that more of the burden of teaching children to read would fall on the junior school.

Some impression of what the schools were like can be gained from what they praised and blamed. They criticized the schools for the sometimes excessive amount of time devoted to subjects like art, music, handicrafts and PE at the expense of 'the study of subjects that were firmly regarded as the backbone of the curriculum'. They favoured more thorough, more interest-based teaching making the most of the close association between school work and life outside school, using varied methods and with 'less talking by the teacher and a more active participation by the child'. The curriculum had to be 'pruned of all irrelevancies'. 'A realistic policy' they declared, 'is the only policy which holds any promise of success for the senior school.'

Comprehensive planning

By the time Mr R. A. Butler came to work on the 1944 Education Act, the day continuation ideas mooted in 1918, the sociological and educational criticisms of the divided post-primary system, and the hopes which were being nourished by the senior elementary schools, came together in the White Paper on *Educational Reconstruction* issued in 1943. (Even before this, Savage, like Blair before him, had in 1940 sent a minute round his senior colleagues 'pointing out,' as Dr A. G. Hughes put it, 'that it was as necessary to prepare for peace as for war'.)

On the basis of the White Paper, the L.C.C. Education Committee set up a sub-committee to lay down the principles on which the authority's secondary school plan should be based. Its report was approved by the Education Committee at the end of July 1944, in a basement meeting place while the flying bombs were falling.

Following the logical development of the principles in the 1935 document, the report came down firmly in favour of a system of multilateral schools in place of the system of separate grammar, central and technical schools, which, it pointed out, had come about only by historical accident. It referred to the American high school – with reserve about its standards – and assumed that ninety large schools, 2,000 strong, would be needed if eighty per cent of the pupils continued to leave at 15.

Four recommendations were put forward:

1. A plan should aim at 'a system of comprehensive high schools throughout the County of London providing for all pupils equal opportunity for physical, intellectual, social and spiritual development . . . full development of personality their first objective'.
2. In a reformed system, there would be 'no place for the senior or modern school differentiated from other types'. Such a school 'would have inferior status . . . [being] . . . solely for those who fail to secure admission elsewhere'.
3. In rebuilding devastated areas 'sites sufficiently large to accommodate a complete cross section of the surrounding post-primary population in one comprehensive unit should be secured'.
4. While new buildings are being built, existing post-primary units should be grouped together so as to form single comprehensive units.

According to a leader in *The Times Educational Supplement*, the scheme could 'truly be described as revolutionary. Bold in conception it proposes a lay-out and organization without precedent in English education.' To which the *Educational Supplement* added its own revolutionary sentiments:

The old world is dead. A new one is painfully struggling to be born. Its life blood is education. . . .

On the issue of multilateralisation versus the segregation of pupils this journal has never held but the one view: that for both social and strictly educational reasons the all-purpose secondary school is to be preferred to the 'type' school.

The overriding importance of the London plan lies, however, not in its details nor even in its organizational outline. It lies in the fact that the greatest municipality in the world has surveyed its educational needs in the field of secondary education with an imaginative yet realistic eye and has not been afraid to draft a scheme which is courageous and far-seeing yet strictly relevant to those needs.

10 *Wartime*

For London schools, the Second World War meant evacuation and the biggest ever disruption of the education system. Mr. G. A. N. Lowndes has described the background to this in the second edition of his *Silent Social Revolution*, drawing in detail on his knowledge as a London assistant education officer on loan to the Ministry of Health after Munich, to overhaul national planning for the evacuation of schools.

London had made full evacuation plans before the 1938 Munich crisis while the Home Office under Sir Samuel Hoare continued to temporize. Lowndes's own administrative experience had included the job of organizing the assembly of 70,000 school children on Constitution Hill and in the Mall to greet the King and Queen on one of the Jubilee drives in 1935, and later he had been responsible for marshalling 37,000 children on the Embankment on Coronation Day, 1937. Both these peace-time logistic exercises had shown him how large numbers of school children under the control of their own teachers could be moved from all points of the London compass by public transport.

It also happened that, twenty-five years before, Lowndes had gone with his father, the rector of a parish on the East coast, to visit the homes of the parishioners, asking for billets for an expected contingent of casualties. The casualties had not, in fact, arrived, but Lowndes had remembered the widespread willingness of ordinary people to take in strangers. This, too, was to be important in planning the response to the threat of bombing.

As the outbreak of war became imminent, the plans were brought to a stand-by stage. Before the summer term ended – on 19 July – a full-scale rehearsal involving 5,000 children and their teachers was carried out in Chelsea. Everything went according to plan apart from minor snags which helped to show what to avoid when the real thing came. On 14 August, the key staff were recalled from holiday. On 25 August, the schools were reassembled, and the plans were tested in the nervous days which followed.

The evacuation order was received on Thursday, 31 August, to be put into operation the following day. London had assumed responsibility for evacuation planning for the whole of the Greater London area, and the Education Department was also responsible for the evacuation of old people and pregnant women. The special schools and nursery schools had their own arrangements with transport to take them to requisitioned holiday camps, country houses and sea-side hotels.

At the last minute the carefully worked out plans were speeded up by the Ministry of Health – a four-day programme telescoped into three – which caused minor chaos. There were 1,589 assembly points, 168 stations from which parties departed, 271 stations where they were set down. The reception areas spanned the whole of Eastern England, the Midlands and the South and West – altogether about 287,000 left the first day and by the morning of the fourth day some 600,000 persons had been moved out of the Greater London area.

Mothers accompanied young children. Other children were on their own in school parties, labelled and carrying their cardboard gas-mask cases in the manner made familiar by the newsreel pictures. All had to be billeted in the homes of families in the reception areas. Almost all the teachers volunteered to take part in the evacuation and the improvisation of schools at the other end. Among those who helped to cope with the myriad of individual problems implied by an operation of this kind were the school nurses and care committee organizers who acted as welfare staff.

Altogether some forty-nine per cent of the London school population – about 200,000 – was dispersed in the first ten days of September. The proportion who stayed behind was significantly bigger than expected. Plans were made on the basis of an eighty per cent evacuation – the percentage suggested by the experience of the 1938 crisis; four out of five of those then eligible had said they would go. The plan had not been carried out in the event because war was averted that time. How many would in fact have gone none could tell. Experience at every subsequent evacuation showed that it was unusual for more than eighty per cent of those who registered for evacuation to turn up. L.C.C. officials became adept at ordering transport on the basis of their own private estimates of the likely response.

The whole complicated operation was carried through with remarkable efficiency. But this efficiency – aided, of course, by the absence of the air raids on account of which the evacuation programme was being put in hand – was soon forgotten in the face of the chorus of complaints which began to come in from the reception areas about the hygiene and conduct of the children.

The impact of 200,000 London school children on the rural areas was predictable but shattering. All the differences between town and country and between class and class were exposed and all of them seemed to focus on the physical cleanliness of the children and their personal habits. As an educational process in itself, the mixing of town and country in this way was often salutary and many lasting friendships and enriching experiences were the result: but there was also the clash of custom and attitude, the conflicts over shared accommodation, the children whom nobody wanted in their homes, the older antagonism between the traditional rural values with the brash and often benighted ignorance of urban slumdom. Above all there were the ubiquitous reports of 'lousy' children and mothers who had no idea how to look after them.

H. C. Dent, whose *Education in Transition* published in 1944 contains a graphic account of the effects of the evacuation on the education service (with many London references), had no doubt that the sociological and cultural shock which middle-class England received at the hands of the evacuees – and the literature and inquiries which it gave rise to – was a potent influence on public opinion, reinforcing the idealistic demands for educational reform with first-hand knowledge of social conditions and attitudes among ordinary town-dwellers.

Under the plan, evacuated secondary schools were attached to secondary schools in the evacuation areas. This worked well, except for the isolated cases where personalities clashed, or when the facilities were severely overstrained. By early autumn, all London secondary schools were operating for something like the normal number of hours each week, although a Board of Education survey in January 1940 showed that, in the country as a whole, one secondary evacuee in seven in the reception areas was out of school.

For the elementary schools, things were a good deal more difficult. They were not working to prearranged plans for links with schools in the reception areas. They had to act on the principle of every man for himself and improvise as best they could. The same Board of Education survey showed that, four months after the outbreak of war, about a quarter of all the evacuated elementary school children were receiving classes neither in school nor at home. Great store was set on retaining the individuality of the London schools in exile. London inspectors continued to visit their schools and any attempt to transfer responsibility for London children to the education authorities in the reception areas was hotly resisted.

From the first, the London education service had to decide what to do about those who remained behind, and those who, in increasing numbers, began to find their way back to London. Usually it was the mothers who first found that they could not bring themselves to endure country life any longer while London remained unattacked. Eighty per cent of the mothers had returned by Christmas. Their children soon followed to join those who ran wild in London streets. One in seven of those who were evacuated were back in a matter of weeks. Without schools for them to go to, they soon got up to mischief, some of them taking up more serious forms of delinquency.

Back in London the prodigies of improvisation had to be achieved without the uncovenanted benefits of country life, and often without teachers or premises. The reopening of London's evening institutes in the winter of 1939, according to Dent, was 'one of the minor epics of the earlier days of the war'. A lavish publicity campaign with posters by Grimes, a famous cartoonist, had been mounted in readiness for the autumn. Air-raid shelters were improvised at the evening institutes with sandbags; students and staff made black-out materials. More than 100 institutes were open by Christmas 1939.

The children who remained in London could not be neglected. Home teaching had to be organized, and from December onwards London had some 'emergency schools' open on a voluntary basis, even though there were inadequate air-raid shelters and the parents had to consent to the risk involved. It was estimated that nearly 200,000 children in London were out of school in December 1939. Against this, the available unoccupied school buildings were only sufficient to provide schooling on a double shift basis for the children aged 11 or over. Not everyone in London was altogether sorry to see the breakdown of the service. There were still parts of London where a reversion to older habits came easily and children out of school meant extra help at home or earlier paid employment.

Before the end of 1939, London teachers, responding to the call for volunteers to return to inner London areas to work under the guidance of the inspectorate, had begun to round up some of the children who were still running wild. Wearing L.C.C. armlets they knocked at doors and scoured the streets, gathering children of school age into centres – not necessarily in school buildings. As word of the emergency classes passed round, children began to turn up of their own accord or were sent by their parents. At first teaching groups were limited to not more than twelve pupils. The next step was to organize emergency classes into emergency schools.

One of the first, in December 1939, opened in the Avenue School for Boys, Walworth, where Mr Leaver, the headmaster, returned from Wonersh, Surrey, where he had been evacuated with a third of his 600 pupils. His emergency school took in boys and girls on a shift basis, with places for 100 in the morning and 100 in the afternoon. Air-raid precautions demanded bricked-up windows and sandbags and air-raid shelters within convenient distance. Even this could be turned to educational advantage in an enterprising school. *The Schoolmaster* in March 1940 carried pictures of the Argyle Emergency School, King's Cross, where the head, Miss Gibson, combined lessons in local geography with a project on the location of nearby air-raid shelters. A huge map of the area was drawn on the floor of the school hall, decorated with flags showing where all the ARP posts were. As the emergency schools assimilated more and more of the children who would otherwise run wild, the demand grew in Parliament and outside that compulsory school attendance, suspended at the outbreak of war, should be reimposed.

In February 1940 the Government reached the same conclusion and instructed local authorities that attendance would again be required from 1 April 1940, by which time London had upwards of 85,000 places open, in 275 emergency schools, backed up by twenty voluntary play centres, created by the initiative of Mrs G. M. Trevelyan and a band of enthusiasts.

The recovery from the first evacuation period was barely completed before the fall of France and the Low Countries and the threat of invasion brought about a second evacuation of London and another suspension of the school attendance laws. On 11 June, all the London schools were closed and 100,000 children began to be moved out. At least half the children of school age stayed behind in London, and the emergency schools had to start again with improved air-raid shelters. Even in wartime there was energy left to argue about who should pay for school air-raid shelters. Should they be grant-aided at the ordinary fifty per cent rate or receive a special 100 per cent Exchequer grant? Delay and wrangling continued till December 1940 when at last the Government agreed to pay the full amount and the schools were equipped with the solid shelters built to Civil Defence standards which continued for too long to grace their playgrounds after the end of the war.

As the bombing built up, more children were evacuated or evacuated themselves, but never anything like all the children of school age: in October 1940 there were still over 100,000 left in London, to share the shelter life of their parents and relations and endure the hardships of the second winter of the war. The emergency schools continued as best they could, serving also as emergency rest centres and places where homeless families could be fed and housed. In the East End the school missions and university settlements performed prodigies of kindness and social assistance, as well as helping to contact and occupy the hundreds of children who stayed out of school.

On 3 December 1940, the L.C.C. announced that, having consulted the Board of Education, they now intended to enforce school attendance again, and a week later all other education authorities were advised to do likewise. London education slowly returned to the wartime normal – partly in the evacuated schools which stayed in the country, partly in those schools in London which had been released by the civil defence and military authorities and which still remained usable in spite of bombing. During periods of heavy night bombing, schooling was liable to be disrupted as buildings were commandeered at short notice to serve as temporary rest centres. Each morning the education officer, Sir Graham Savage, would find on his desk a return showing the result of the previous night's raid: immediately, the emergency services would be in operation diverting the children to other schools.

The unalterable verities of the educational year were maintained – children still sat for junior county secondary scholarships and the 11 plus continued to operate under bizarre conditions, thanks to close cooperation between the evacuation and the reception areas. Children, by and large, continued to go to the evacuated grammar schools which they would have attended had there been no war. This could easily mean that the child whose elementary school was evacuated to Yarmouth had to be 're-evacuated' at 11 to Cornwall for secondary schooling.

Back in London, a dozen emergency grammar schools provided for those who passed the scholarship examination. These pupils, too, retained a link with their 'local' grammar schools: each emergency school included groups of children who, notionally, belonged to different named local grammar schools, and who would expect to revert to their 'own' schools after 'the duration'.

All the upheavals of evacuation and emergency schooling, the departure of staff on active service, and the disruption of normal family life, took a predictable toll of educational standards, as post-war surveys of basic subjects showed. In 1943 the London inspectorate carried out their own survey among 13-year-olds in four major subjects – English, arithmetic, history and geography. They had the greatest difficulty in interpreting the results but the general inference to be drawn was that there was an average set-back of six to twelve months. In July 1944, after months of comparative quiet, when more and more evacuees had returned to London, came the flying bombs and V2 rockets and another round of evacuation. By this time the education service was more experienced in the arts of improvisation, and the routine was put into operation once more. With much of Southern England under threat of attack, evacuees had to go father afield; many went to Lancashire and the North-West. When at last the time came for the last evacuees to return, some 290 London schools had been destroyed or seriously damaged, 310 more had been extensively but less seriously damaged. Only fifty schools out of 1,200 escaped scot free.

In spite of the well-publicized difficulties, the evidence of dirt and squalor, the notorious dirty heads and skin diseases, many of the evacuees had been taken warmly into the hearts of their foster parents, and ended the war with two homes instead of one. Occasionally evidence of this filters through to the files in the record room at County Hall where the documentary evidence of the evacuation is stored, in letters like that from a lady in Liskeard who fostered thirty-three evacuees in six years of war. She wrote to the education officer in July 1945 for permission to travel to London at her own expense to make sure her family of six children from Forest Hill – including 'Bunny aged seven who is not a good traveller' and Brian her twin brother, 'a fair imp' – got home safely.

Part three *1944-70*

11 *The educational explosion*

Anyone confronted with the remarkable record of the last quarter of a century's growth in London education might be excused if he felt that it defies brief synoptic description.

It threatens, also, to overwhelm the century's perspective, overshadowing the rest of the story since 1870, because of the sheer size of the education service which has been created since 1944.

The perspective is important, however, for there is a sense in which the rapid growth of the post-war period needs to be seen as a continuation of a normal condition of growth which characterized London education between 1870 and 1914 – and within which the interwar years (notwithstanding their undervalued achievements) appear as no more than a frustrating interlude.

To argue this way, however, is not to belittle the 1944 Education Act, or to minimize the developments which have flowed from it – nor yet the revolution in personal aspirations – which have caused the true explosion of education and brought a rising proportion of the population within the network of secondary, further and higher education, and kept them in it longer.

Some indication of the transformation all this has brought about in London schools and colleges can be obtained from a crude statistical comparison of 1946 and 1968. In 1945–6 London spent £14·4 million on education; by 1970 this had risen to £143·5 million.

The way in which the increase is broken down illustrates how the balance of educational activity has changed. In 1945–6 primary education accounted for £4·8 million – a third of the total. In 1970, however, when primary education cost £26 million, it only accounted for about eighteen per cent of the whole bill.

Secondary education, on the other hand, grew faster and consumed a slightly bigger share; in 1945–6 it cost £2·9 million (about twenty per cent), whereas by 1970 this had gone up to £32 million, or twenty-two per cent.

At the upper end, spending on further and higher education is up from £1·3 million to £25 million – that is from less than ten per cent of the total to about seventeen per cent, while teacher training which cost £88,000 in 1945–6 (about 0·6 per cent) has jumped to £4.8 million (rather more than three per cent).

This shows the pattern of development. The primary schools have been reorganized and primary education has been transformed, but by the time the 1944 Act was passed the elementary schools already provided a service of universal primary education.

	1945–6	1970–71
Total	£14,443,800	£143,507,000
Amount to be met from Rates	£6,931,000	£89,670,000
Primary	£4,841,000	£25,972,000
Secondary	£2,897,000	£32,005,000
Special	£455,300	£4,536,000
Further and Higher	£1,286,800	£24,969,000
Training of teachers	£88,000	£4,781,000
Milk, meals	£935,000	£8,549,000
New items since 1946		
Careers service		£594,000
Educational TV service		£610,000
Service of Youth		£1,582,000

Secondary education, however, was still very much a minority pursuit in 1945, and, though the 1944 Act raised the school-leaving age and nominally guaranteed 'secondary education for all', the quarter of a century since the Act has been devoted to giving the slogan reality. Progress in this direction is now clearly measured by the growth during the 1950s and 1960s of those who voluntarily stay beyond the leaving age. And while, between 1946 and 1968, the secondary school population has grown by a third, from 122,000 to 164,000, the number of full-time students in further and higher education has multiplied by nearly four, rising from 13,800 to 42,300 since 1950.

Pupils Staying on After Statutory Leaving Age (Percentages)

Year	15+	16+	17+	18+
1952	34·0	12·9		
1953	35·3	13·7	4·9	1·6
1963	52·32	20·28	10·22	2·01
1964	54·89	22·37	10·43	2·25
1965	57·42	24·95	11·97	1·97
1966	59·42	27·07	13·76	2·83
1967	62·74	30·14	15·48	2·79
1968	64·56	31·81	17·02	2·93
1969	65·58	33·22	17·60	3·14

Five years before the centenary of the 1870 Act, London's educational administration underwent a third change of direction. The L.C.C., which had taken over responsibility for education in 1904, was abolished in 1965 under the London Government Act of 1963. The Greater London Council which took over most of the L.C.C.'s former functions did not become the education authority. Attempts, reminiscent of those in 1902 and 1903, were made to divide responsibility for education between the London boroughs and the G.L.C. (as recommended by the Herbert Commission), but the combined resistance of the London education service and the Ministry of Education prevented the break-up of London as an education area, and with a few minor, tidying, adjustments the education service for London continued to be provided over the area originally drawn up for the Metropolitan Board of Works in the middle of the last century.

The new education authority for London, the Inner London Education Authority, was, technically, a special committee of the G.L.C., whose members were made up of forty G.L.C. councillors representing the twelve inner London boroughs and the City of London, and thirteen members appointed by the borough councils of the inner London boroughs and the City. The I.L.E.A. works through an education committee to which up to nineteen additional members are appointed. Finance is raised by a precept on the inner London boroughs and the City of London.

After the change of administration structure, certain technical services formerly provided by the L.C.C. passed to the G.L.C. – for example, the architect's department – on which the I.L.E.A. Education Committee has continued to rely. The school medical service was reorganized with the borough medical officers of health acting as I.L.E.A. principal school medical officers for their areas.

The London plan

The man on whom the main responsibility for London's response to the 1944 Act fell in the immediate post-war period was Graham Savage, education officer from 1940 to 1951. When Rich announced his retirement, Savage was senior chief inspector at the Board of Education. He was a Cambridge science graduate who had entered the secondary school inspectorate immediately after the First World War and made his way to the top. At fifty-four he faced retirement within six years if he stayed at the Board of Education. Not only was the London job a challenge which appealed to him, it also carried twice the chief inspector's salary. To clinch matters the Board of Education was about to be evacuated to Bournemouth and Savage, having seen two-thirds of his H.M.I.s seconded to other Government duties, saw no real job to do for the duration of the war if he stayed with the Board.

He took over in July 1940 at the height of the second evacuation and carried the brunt of the war years, working very closely with the chairman, Charles Robertson, with whom he shared a common experience – both had worked in the Egyptian education service before the First World War. Robertson was a widely respected figure, quiet, sympathetic, kindly – 'too kind sometimes' in the face of heated wartime arguments about the shape of London's post-war education. Savage was the author of London's multilateral secondary scheme – he did not recall ever reading the 1935 report which prefigured its essential principles – but he made it his business, through Robertson, to be sensitive to the discussion going on in the majority party throughout this period.* (It was at a party group meeting that a new member, Harold Shearman, chairman of the education committee from 1955 to 1961, suggested the adoption of the term 'comprehensive' as a felicitous alternative to multilateral.)

Savage's deputy (and successor) was Dr John Brown who, at the time of Rich's retirement, was L.C.C. chief inspector. Savage and Brown made a formidable and very different pair. Savage came in from outside like a breath of needed fresh air. He wanted to limit the power of the London inspectorate; as an H.M.I. he had discovered how much of the work normally carried out by H.M.I.s elsewhere had by convention been delegated in London to the L.C.C. inspectorate. He distrusted the peculiar combination of administrative and advisory duties which fell to the London inspectorate. Teachers, he felt, were too dependent for their promotion on the goodwill of the inspectors which was necessary to get on to the promotion list.

Brown as senior chief inspector resisted this, and Savage never succeeded fully in his plans to reorganize the L.C.C. inspection system. Brown's continuing concern, as deputy and later as education officer, was to weld and hold together the London teaching service, and to prove that a large authority did not have to be impersonal in its relations with its teachers. Though he and Savage often did not see eye to eye, in reality they complemented each other. Savage was the innovator, the man whose reaction to a new idea was more likely to be positive. Brown, the canny Scot, took

---

* He was greatly assisted by Dr A. G. Hughes, L.C.C. Chief Inspector of Schools.

more impressing. When Tawney was brought in as expert adviser by the Labour group in 1934, Brown was assistant education officer for secondary education. He had been the man who had the thankless task of keeping the committee's feet on the ground. 'Everything I recommend,' said Tawney, 'John Brown proves is too expensive or impractical.' Tawney's patience with committees was quickly expended.

When John Brown succeeded Savage as education officer in 1951, W. F. Houghton, then deputy education officer for Birmingham, was appointed in Brown's place, taking up his duties in the following year. In 1956 he was appointed education officer on Brown's retirement. He received a knighthood in 1967. The fifth of Sir Robert Blair's successors, he has reigned as administrative head of the London education service longer than any man since Blair, and during the period in which London education has expanded most rapidly, his influence has been correspondingly extensive. Although throughout these years education has always been near the centre of London's political strife, Houghton has succeeded in retaining the trust and respect of both the political parties which have controlled the L.C.C. and the I.L.E.A. during his term of office, while at the same time defending the integrity of the professional advice which the education authority has received.

The London School Plan was prepared between 1944 and 1947. It formulated London's complete scheme of primary and secondary schools on the best information then available. The estimated cost at 1947 prices came to £187 million, with another £29 million for the further education scheme.

To prepare the plan, there had to be a meticulous review of the whole London school scene, with an assessment of the expected child population and the sites and buildings available and required. 'Nothing less than a root and branch operation' would do. The existing council elementary schools were built on sites which averaged one acre. Voluntary schools made do with about one-quarter of the area. The new building regulations demanded two or three acres for primary schools, and three acres or more for secondary.

Much of the planning had to be speculative in that the future demography of the London area could not be foretold with certainty. Would the birth rate revert to the pre-war level? Would there continue to be emigration by Londoners to the outer suburbs? These were as much unknowns as the immigration from overseas into London which was to be a feature of the 1950s and 1960s.

In the comprehensive secondary proposals the plan was influenced by current thinking which assumed that no school could provide an adequate range of ability unless it included at least three forms of 'grammar-type' entry. In London this implied thirteen or fourteen forms of entry. The theory behind this was derived from the practical experience of the time that the sixth forms of grammar schools were drawn from only the top two streams. As patterns of staying on have changed, the required size of comprehensives has been scaled down, but the first examples, such as Kidbrooke and Woodberry Down, were based on the earlier assumptions.

From the first the planners were confronted with the entrenched position of the aided grammar schools. Repeatedly during the early post-war years London's educational leaders sought ways of pressing them to fall in with the comprehensive policy. The matter was discussed formally and informally with Ministers in the Government between 1945 and 1951, but the legal position remained unchanged and the education committee had to accept what to the majority was the anomaly of a comprehensive secondary scheme which included the retention of fifty-five aided grammar schools.

In the early years the Conservatives, led by Dame Catherine Fulford, kept up a running fight against the comprehensive plan. They did not attack the comprehensive school in principle but argued that, rather than embark on a full-scale comprehensive plan, the L.C.C. should start with a modest pilot project. They also stood firmly beside the aided grammar schools and defended their choice to stay outside the scheme.

What would have happened if the Conservatives had won the London election in 1949 can only be guessed. London went to the polls a matter of hours after Sir Stafford Cripps introduced an austerity budget, and there was a massive swing against the Labour Party. The vote produced an equal number of Labour and Conservative members with one Liberal, Sir Percy Harris, with the effective casting vote, which he used to help Labour retain control.

While these matters were being debated, there were other, more pressing things to be attended to. As the schools came back into use, they had to be redecorated and repaired. Bomb damage had to be restored. Schools had to be restocked with books. Furniture which had followed evacuees to improvised schools from Norfolk to Cornwall had to be recovered. Major and minor building programmes had from the start to be geared to immediate needs, including provision for the extra children who would have to stay in school when the leaving age went up in 1947.

No sooner had the secondary schools absorbed the extra age group than the birth-rate bulge of 1947–8 promised extra numbers in the primary schools. Working against a background of economic stringency and shortage of building materials, London managed to put up sixty-six new school buildings between 1948 and 1954 and rebuild fifty severely war-damaged schools, thereby creating in all some 43,000 school places, to which were added 2,000 more in prefabricated huts.

Along with these programmes went a string of minor improvements – including the replacement of outdoor sanitation and the removal of 'stepping' from 2,000 class rooms which still had desks raked in rows from the time when a teacher had to be able to see, and be seen by, a class of sixty or seventy children. Many of the schools which continued in use were substantial buildings dating back to the School Board days, and many of them needed a lot of renovation. In 1946 it was decided to install electricity in the 326 L.C.C. schools which were still lit by gas.

To go with the new building and renovation there were extensive re-equipment and refurnishing programmes – in the five years to 1954, £1·5 million for furniture, £340,000 for visual and aural aids, £150,000 for other equipment. More than £1 million was spent on Government surplus equipment for science laboratories and workshops.

As the school building programme gathered momentum the process of rehousing London's children in new and modernized schools went forward. Between 1954 and 1957, sixteen new primary schools and twenty-five new secondary schools came into use and a total of 7,200 primary and 29,000 secondary places were provided. In the next five years to 1962, twenty-four primary schools and thirty-two new, enlarged or rebuilt secondary schools were completed – a total of 7,900 primary and 32,200 secondary places.

A full account of the history of London education at this period would have to tell of the ingenuity of the architects, working within strict cost limits, under the guidance of the design analysis undertaken by the Ministry of Education's Architectural Development Group, and the way they increased the value obtained for the large sums of money laid out. The key to this was the attempt to marry the educational and architectural planning in such a way as to provide buildings most economically adapted to their teaching function. As pedagogic methods changed – at first, more especially in the primary schools – the design of the schools changed and the interior layout became more flexible, in line with more informal teaching arrangements.

A comparison of the design of some early post-war primary schools with an outstanding modern design such as the Evelyn Lowe School at Camberwell – or at the secondary level, a comparison of the formal masses of the Kidbrooke design with the new Pimlico school – provides physical evidence of the changes.

One factor in the process of architectural development has been the sheer size of the programmes and the experience which this has enabled architects, administrators, inspectors and teachers, to build up in London, as elsewhere. During the School Board period, the evolution of the school building from the primitive groupings of class rooms to the majestic self-confidence of the traditional London three-decker represented just such a combination of educational and architectural experience over a prolonged period of large-scale building.

One constant feature of the London scene was this contrast between the old and the new – between the standards demanded by the new building regulations and the standards tolerated in the old buildings. At no time in the post-war period has it been possible to postpone new development till the backlog of old and unsatisfactory buildings have been replaced. Always there has been the contrast between the generous aspiration for the future, summed up in brand new schools, and the make-do-and-mend which has patched up old buildings.

Inevitably, the principle of 'roofs over heads' – the priority needs of rising and mobile populations – has had to govern the building pro-grammes. This has meant that new housing estates have had priority over run-down inner city areas. The schools have had to go where the population is, and latter-day administrators, like their School Board predecessors, have noted empty places in schools which need to be replaced, and smart new schools which are overcrowded before they have opened.

Throughout the period under the minor works programme attempts have been made to improve the old buildings which must continue to be used. New staff rooms, new lavatories, improved playgrounds – all these have been provided in many schools, together with the kind of facelifts which painting and decorating can give. But the contrast has remained, to be highlighted in the Newsom and Plowden reports, and to provide one of the reasons for a policy of 'positive discrimination' and the new statement of old objectives comprised by the 'educational priority area' concept. Many of the more intractable problems, however, can only be tackled by the operation of a long-term plan: many schools on restricted sites can only be satisfactorily renovated, given more space – which means waiting for a new school – and there remain the practical questions to ask about how much money it is worth spending on schools which are scheduled to be replaced altogether in the near future.

Other developments

As well as attending to the basic needs of the schools, the L.C.C. had to interpret the broader intentions of the 1944 Act. In many respects this meant pressing forward with the kind of developments which had already begun in less enlightened times. The change-over from elementary to primary education meant strengthening the work among junior children and encouraging the use of more informal methods of modifying the internal arrangement of the schools. School libraries were not in themselves new, but a beginning was made in providing better libraries in non-selective schools to bring them nearer to what had become accepted in grammar schools. Primary schools were helped to build up class-room libraries and book corners. From 1947 onwards, there was financial aid to school clubs and societies – activities which had long been a recognized part of school life, but which were now raised in importance and stimulated on a wider scale. The L.C.C. began to pay for affiliation fees for schools to join athletic, music, drama and similar associations. School visits – which had begun back in the School Board days – visits to the theatre, opera, and to concerts, educational journeys of all kinds, all benefited from a more generous approach.

Wartime experience of farming and forestry camps had shown the educational value of short-term boarding of various kinds. Use was made of the permanent camps run by the National Camps Corporation. When this organization was wound up, London acquired two of the camp sites in Surrey – at Hindhead and at Ewhurst – and, in the course of time, to these have been added a camp in Dorset and a mountain centre in North Wales.

Other forms of boarding education (in addition to special schools) also came up for consideration in the light of the new Act. In 1946 a scheme was introduced to provide up to £100,000 a year for boarding grants to children who had some recognizable need to go away to school. In 1951, the L.C.C. set up its own boarding school – to augment, not replace, the boarding grants – at Woolverstone Hall, near Ipswich. With additional buildings, this was expanded to take a total of 360 boys. A boarding house was provided at Crown Woods, a comprehensive school in south-east London, for 120 boys and girls, as part of a scheme to provide boarding places for service families.

Music teaching flourished in the more liberal atmosphere. The authority began to provide musical instruments and widen the range of musical activities for those with exceptional musical ability by organizing holiday courses under the senior inspector of music. Out of this came the London Schools Symphony Orchestra and a succession of public concerts in London and abroad. School drama activities benefited from the acquisition in 1959 of a fine collection of theatrical costumes – kept at the School Equipment Centre for loan to schools. In 1964 the Toynbee Theatre, Stepney, was taken over as a drama centre for the London education service, to be augmented by the Jeannetta Cochrane Theatre in 1964 and in 1970 by a purpose-built Youth Arts Centre at Gateforth Street, Paddington.

The unification of secondary education highlighted the gap between the standards of social provision for the grammar schools and the rest. Most of the grammar schools had their own playing fields. To provide playing fields for the rest of the secondary school population it was necessary to develop land in the Green Belt, and create sports centres to which pupils from the inner areas could be transported by bus. The first (in 1955) was at Morden Park, Surrey, where eighty-one acres provided facilities for about 8,000 children. By 1970 the number of sports centres had risen to 10 covering 600 acres and providing for some 55,000 pupils each week. Each has a resident educational supervisor – a qualified PE teacher.

Three major developments under the Education Act extended the range of the education authority's activities. The School Meals Service was made an integral part of educational provision – no longer regarded as a special service for the relief of need, but as an ordinary social service – and in London provided by a separate L.C.C. department, responsible to the Education Committee for school meals.

The youth service, boosted during the war by a recognition of the needs of young people awaiting call-up, became a general responsibility of local education authorities under the 1944 Act. Already in 1940 a London Youth Committee had been formed to coordinate the activities of a wide range of voluntary organizations, many of which ran clubs which the L.C.C. aided. In 1943 the first four youth organizers were appointed to the staff of London divisions, followed by others in 1944 and 1946.

Working within narrow financial limits, the policy was to make school

premises available for youth activities and to offer grants to the voluntary
organizations through which the bulk of the work continued to be done.
The L.C.C. also ran recreational institutes for young people within the
further education service.

Following the Albemarle Report in 1959, the whole programme was
reviewed and expanded, grants to voluntary youth organizations jumping
from £56,000 a year between 1957 and 1960, to £220,000 in 1961–2, and
£266,000 in 1962–3. In 1960 a principal county youth organizer was
appointed. In seven years, London was able to authorize £2 million worth
of building – rather more than half by voluntary organization, and the
rest in the shape of purpose-built specialist sport and art centres, school-
based youth centres, an outdoor pursuits centre and fifteen mixed clubs
in under-provided areas where voluntary organizations were unable to go
ahead.

In the course of time, also, the philosophy of youth service has become
more 'youth-centred' and less organization-centred – youth work has
come to be regarded as the provision of a wide range of activities and
opportunities to meet the needs of individual young people, and less as a
matter of enrolling them in this corporate group or that.

In 1949, London decided to exercise the option open under the
Employment and Training Act of 1948 to organize the Youth Employment
Service in the London area. Some nineteen (later increased to twenty)
youth employment bureaux were set up and the advisory service extended
to cover those in full-time education beyond 16, taking over the work
formerly done by the London Headmasters' and Headmistresses' Employment Committees.

The conception of a youth employment service has changed over the
twenty-year period since 1949. It has remained a service with responsibility
both to industry and to the schools, in which the interests of the individual
pupil have remained paramount, but the absence of juvenile unemployment and the tendency to stay on at school beyond the minimum leaving
age have put increasing emphasis on careers guidance and counselling.

Meanwhile, of course, the tasks of placement and replacement have
continued, together with other duties in connection with the national
insurance legislation. Increasingly, however, the work of Careers Officers
(as youth employment officers were subsequently re-christened) has
depended on close cooperation with the schools where careers teaching
has begun to appear as a subject on the timetables.

By 1970 the careers service had entered its own period of uncertainty and reappraisal as the Department of Employment and Productivity pondered plans for a national advisory service under its own auspices.

Teachers

Like the rest of the country, in the post-war period London was acutely conscious of the shortage of teachers, the more so as the Minister of Education had, in 1945, introduced new staffing regulations making forty the maximum number of children for primary classes and thirty for secondary. There was, from the start, an element of bluff in these figures which have yet to be achieved nationally.

As an education authority, London has always been attractive to teachers. But throughout the period there were various national quota systems in operation designed to help the less attractive areas. So the numbers of over-size classes mounted, first in the primary schools, and then in the secondary schools, as the post-war baby bulge worked its way through the system.

One answer was to train more teachers. Six emergency training colleges were set up by London under the national scheme at the end of the war, many of whose students went on to teach in London schools.

In the context of the early 1950s, the teacher shortage looked like a temporary phenomenon. There were confident predictions (never shared by representatives of London) that by 1960 the teacher shortage would be over. It was on the basis of these predictions that the college of education course was extended to three years. By then, however, changed social customs had raised the 'wastage' rate for the teaching profession, and in the face of earlier marriage and retirement for child-rearing by young women teachers, the colleges of education had to be further expanded throughout the 1960s. Only as 1970 approached did it begin to look as if the supply of, and demand for, teachers was coming into balance.

Special schools

The return from evacuation and the 1944 Act combined to make a full-scale review of special education an immediate necessity. Care for the handicapped had been an early preoccupation of the School Board and this had continued under the L.C.C. But handicaps did not remain the same. Some, like tuberculosis, were relieved by improvements in physical health.

Others, like those of the maladjusted child, came to the fore in the light of increasing knowledge and changed attitudes.

From 1930 onwards, London had been responsible for schools and children's homes formerly administered by the Poor Law Guardians. These had added to the boarding establishments which came under the L.C.C. taking their place alongside very different institutions for the blind and deaf and mentally defective. The full range included children's homes, remand homes, Approved schools, reception homes, open-air schools and schools for the mentally and physically handicapped.

Wartime experience had shown the value of boarding schools for many of the handicapped children. Evacuation had, perforce, taken many children away from their homes to schools and hostels in the country and it was felt that there were a number of children whose physical and mental condition were best treated away from home, and away from domestic circumstances which contributed to their social difficulties.

Before plans could be put into effect to double the number of boarding special school places which, after war damage and loss, stood in 1946 at about 850, an incident occurred at Marlesford Lodge, Hammersmith, which caused widespread concern. Marlesford Lodge was an ex-poor law institution to which girls from a remand home were temporarily transferred. The girls rioted in circumstances which were examined in detail by a Home Office inquiry. The report was critical of the L.C.C., whose embarrassment was compounded by harsh and – as many people thought – unjustified criticisms from several stipendiary magistrates. Out of the L.C.C.'s own inquiry and reappraisal came the decision to appoint an inspector with special concern for residential establishments – Miss D. A. Plastow – who, two years later, in 1949, became assistant education officer for special education and till her retirement in 1967, helped to carry through the re-shaping of the London Special Education Service.

It was not possible at this period to build new boarding schools. So the first thing to do was to search for existing buildings which could be taken over and adapted. Three country houses and a large hutted camp, used during the war, were retained and adapted, and eighteen more country houses were acquired in the seven years which followed the preparation of the London School Plan. Each house needed a good deal of adaptation ('often enough the houses were of limited value but it's surprising what you can do with some good stables'). By the time the adaptation had been carried out, the L.C.C. had fashioned a new range of boarding schools, including altogether new provision for maladjusted children. In addition, of course, places were taken at independent special schools. By 1970, the number of boarding special schools had risen to twenty-eight compared with the eleven which existed in 1939.

New approaches to residential care called for new attitudes on the part of the teaching and welfare staff – a more homely atmosphere in school, for example – the staff and the children took their meals together and the last vestiges of Victorian institutionalism were swept away. Maladjusted children presented special difficulties and needed to be looked after in small schools and with the right mixture of patience, kindliness and firmness. The old idea of the open-air school gave way to much less spartan schools for delicate children like Warnham Court, Horsham – a house which turned out to have dry rot, which caused considerable embarrassment to the administrators.

Although the first post-war need was to step up the scale of boarding provision and to provide for maladjusted boarders, as time passed the value of keeping the handicapped child in his own home environment and if possible in an ordinary school gained recognition and much of the later development was in day special schools for educationally subnormal and maladjusted children, and in special classes attached to ordinary schools. Boarding schools – twenty-eight of them – have remained a necessary part of a comprehensive service for handicapped children, for handicaps which are suffered only by few children – for example, the blind – and therefore can only justify a few schools; and for other handicaps which are so severe that they need highly specialized full-time care. But when day schools can cope, or where special classes can allow the children to remain members of an ordinary school community, the prevailing view has been that this has obvious advantages, including that of being less expensive.

Altogether ten categories of handicapped pupils are laid down in the regulations made under the Education Act. These are: blind, partially sighted, deaf, partially hearing, educationally subnormal, epileptic, maladjusted, physically handicapped, speech defects and delicate. To meet these needs there were, by 1970, sixty-six day special schools, twenty-eight boarding schools and six hospital special schools. Many pupils, of course, come within more than one category and some schools specialize in the needs of children with two or more forms of handicap. Some two hundred children are taught in six hospital special schools, and in addition to the special schools and the special classes attached to ordinary schools, a home tuition service provides for boys and girls suffering from physical conditions which prevent them from going to school at all.

A continuing feature of the London special services has been the work of the voluntary care committees, the successors to the well-intentioned voluntary workers whom Robert Blair marshalled before the First World War. The value of their work has been to provide the kind of informal support and help which is needed by handicapped children and their families on a scale which a professional staff of limited size could never offer. But the voluntary care committees have to fit into an increasingly professional background, and the attempt to raise the general standard of care provided by the welfare services has made it necessary to review the relationship between the various agencies which service the handicapped.

As 1970 approached, London prepared for the reorganization of the school care service – following a report prepared by a team at Bedford College, London – and in this the traditional role of the voluntary care committee workers will be modified, to prevent what has always been intended to be an ancillary service from coming between the welfare and care committee staff and the children and families they serve.

12 *New primary schools*

Most people would probably say that it has been in the primary schools that the most interesting post-war educational developments have taken place. It has been here that the continuing tension between 'formal' and 'progressive' ideas has been most clearly seen in practical terms – that is, in actual changes in the way children and teachers spend their time, the things they do, the transactions which take place between them and the environment in which they work.

Many of the ideas and much of the practice go back a long way; much of the theory and the philosophy is fairly shaky, as critics have not hesitated to point out. But, at its pragmatic best, the modern primary school shows more clearly, perhaps, than any other kind of school, the changes in aim and direction in education over the past century, the changed attitude towards children as individual human beings, the contrast in the assumed role of the teacher and the nature of the teacher's authority, the attempt to make schools places where children can freely learn and grow.

Many of these changes relate to attitudes and values and cannot be assessed simply in terms of measurable tasks which children can perform. Where achievement can be measured in subjects like reading and mathematics the evaluation demands complex information about the human resources which go into the schools as well as the specific measured results which come out – hence the controversy which has surrounded the literacy survey published by the Inner London Education Authority in 1970, and the long-term comparisons of results in certain basic subjects reported by Sir Cyril Burt in the *Irish Educational Journal* about the same time.

All this has invested the modern primary school with its full share of controversy – including controversy at a purely technical level between psychologists who differ about testing techniques and the interpretation of such psychometric evidence as comes to light.

It can certainly be said that standards of achievement in basic subjects have risen during the post-war period. But it has also to be conceded that wartime disruption had set back average standards, and, therefore, that progress since the war has included catching up on ground which had been lost. To complicate the issue, the arrival of immigrants, many of whom have language and other learning difficulties, has changed the school population in important respects. Other movements of population suggest that the composition of London schools may also be changing in other ways – that those who move away from the centre to suburbs and new towns outside the metropolitan area may include more of the more intelligent than of the less intelligent.

To interpret standards of attainment, all these changes need to be quantified. And even then, what can be assessed is not the quality of schooling, but one limited aspect of that quality, measured in strictly limited ways. In other respects, the aims of the schools are more difficult to set down in forms which lend themselves to evaluation – not least because they are pluralistic and possibly sometimes in conflict with each other, differing in important respects from school to school and from head teacher to head teacher.

Changes in pedagogic methods in London primary schools have taken place against a background of general development, gathering momentum in the 1960s as the immediate post-war pressure of numbers relaxed, staffing standards improved and changes in the methods of selection for secondary education removed some of the pressures which had formerly borne heavily on the junior schools.

Over the quarter of a century which followed the Second World War, the primary school population rose and fell with the birth-rate trends. In 1945 there were 150,000 primary school children (an artificially depressed figure). By 1969 this had become 247,000. In the years between, it rose as high as 283,000 in 1954 under the full impact of the bulge.

During the same period some 60,000 new primary school places were provided, for the most part to put roofs over the heads of the additional children and match the movement of population. In view of the long-term decline in London's school population since the 1920s, the shortage of places was relative rather than absolute – new housing demanded new schools in new places while old and depressing buildings had to continue to be used in many of the areas from which people were moving out. From 1962 onwards a few major remodelling projects found their way into building programmes – the first major scheme was at the Gateway Primary

School, St Marylebone, a school built in 1887, where, for £56,000, a complete renovation was carried out for half the cost of a new school.

But by 1964, when the L.C.C. gave evidence to the Plowden Committee on Primary Education (and carried out a major review of London primary schools on which to base its written submission), only twelve pre-war schools had been approved for replacement out of a total of 769. The evidence dwelt at some length on the difficulties arising from the need to continue to use unsatisfactory school buildings. Though sanitary improvements had been included in every minor works programme, it was still reckoned that £5 million was needed to replace outdoor lavatories.

The improvement of facilities – and changes in the design of new schools – was closely linked to the new developments in teaching methods. Most schools had begun to make increasing use of project methods and discovery techniques in which the child was encouraged to find out for himself from a rich variety of learning materials accessible to him in the school as a whole and by visits outside the school. Better school libraries and form libraries made this more of a reality, together with such L.C.C. services as the Nature Study Scheme – successor to the original 'botany scheme' started in 1905 – which supplies the schools with plant specimens and also with pets such as rabbits, mice, hamsters and guinea pigs. Increasingly, too – and especially at the infants' stage – more time was devoted to activities chosen by the children themselves to release and canalize their own desire to learn. The same quest for interest and learning through experience could be seen in 'the integrated day' which, in a minority of London junior schools, was leading to the fusion of separate subjects such as history, geography and science into double study periods in which topics could be followed which crossed subject barriers. Examples quoted by the L.C.C. inspectors included the linking of religious education with art, music and drama, the introduction of 'local studies' combining geography with history, science and civics, the relationship of art and craft to most other subjects, and exciting ways in which drama, music and physical education could be combined.

The L.C.C. evidence to Plowden summed up the official attitude towards the new primary education. The tone was that of cautious but determined liberalism. Five main principles were advanced as the basis of the modern methods:

1. *The importance of experience* – Much knowledge, especially at the early stages, should come from experience, both first-hand and less directly through

visual and other media. To this must be added knowledge derived from information. But words or symbols alone have meaning only if the child can interpret them realistically and the teacher should therefore seek all possible means of enlarging his pupils' experience;

2. *The importance of self-reliance* – The child must learn to set his own experience in order and to add to it information derived from other people's experience. In doing this, he both requires and develops basic skills in the use of number and the spoken and written word. He requires too the physical and social self-reliance which the school can give him through modern physical education and through the whole atmosphere and activity of the school;

3. *The importance of motives* – Children do better when they are keen to do and to succeed in what they are set to do. Among the significant and beneficial motives which teachers should seek to harness are the following:
   (a) *Intrinsic interest* – Children are interested in many things for their own sakes. The teacher must seek to identify such things and to choose subject-matter and methods of teaching accordingly;
   (b) *A sense of purpose* – Children are prepared to work hard at something which in itself is uninteresting, if doing so has a purpose which for them is worth while. Moreover, the purpose invoked need not be entirely personal, for the social purpose of the group may become part of the personal motives of its members – an experience itself of great value in social training;
   (c) *Achievement and mastery* – This motive is now widely recognized as of great importance. It indicates the very careful grading of tasks, especially in reading and number, so that each step is just within the child's capability; he is not defeated, and success reinforces learning. Collective pride in a group achievement is similarly important; and
   (d) *Choice* – Children tend to like what they choose to do as well as choosing what they like to do. They will often work very hard at a self-chosen task, just because it is self-chosen;

4. *The importance of integration* – There is need to achieve a proper measure of integration of the curriculum, both as between the information subjects and between these and the basic skills, while at the same time recognizing that children must acquire certain basic skills and knowledge which they need for the future;

5. *The importance of planning and records* – It must be recognized that whether in a 'progressive' school where methods are active, timetable-free, and schemes of work are suggestive rather than mandatory, or in a more formal school, the work should be guided by an overall plan of campaign and that

School design reflects the changes in primary education and the trend towards more informal methods.

Top Group work within a single class enables children to get on with their own chosen work. Middle Row Primary School, 1969.   *Bottom* Split-level class room at the Vittoria School, Islington (designed by the Architectural Development group of the Department of Education and Science). (*The Times*)

Right A scene at a London railway station a few days before the outbreak of the Second World War. A party of London elementary-school children set off for the country.

Part of a letter by a girl evacuated with Camden High School to Uppingham. Being away for the first time means a weekly letter home.

This letter is very
long.

C⁄o Mrs Goodacre
High Street
Uppingham
Rutland.

Dear Mummy & Daddy,
I received your parcel very kind of you to send it and someone must know I like chocolate. I shall absoultly count the days until I see you and Auntie and then I shall only see you for a day or a little more, but if you like the place where you stay perhaps you could stay a little longer, because I could get the time off from school. I know you will think me very selfish, only I am longing to see you, but don't think I am unhappy, Oh no I am very happy only it is very funny without you.
We have to take our gas-masks to school they *do* get in the way. I have sent a postcard to Miss Peck Grannie and Annette. Have you

Top left Practical work can
include domestic science for
boys: a cookery exercise for
boys at Gipsy Road Elementary
School, 1942.
Bottom left Third-formers in
the brickwork shop at a
technical institute.

Top right In the machine
shop at Eltham Green School,
Woolwich, 1956. As the new
comprehensive schools come
into use, they incorporate the
work formerly done in the
technical schools.
Bottom right Sixth-form
biology at Sir Walter St John's
School, 1962.

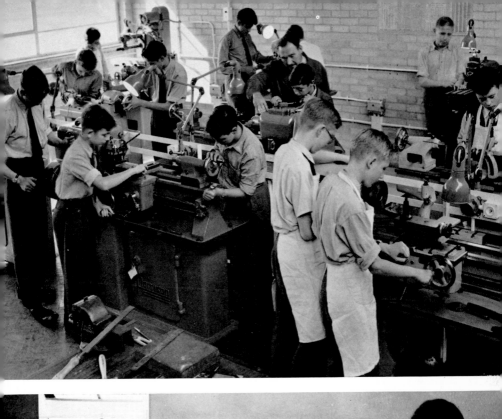
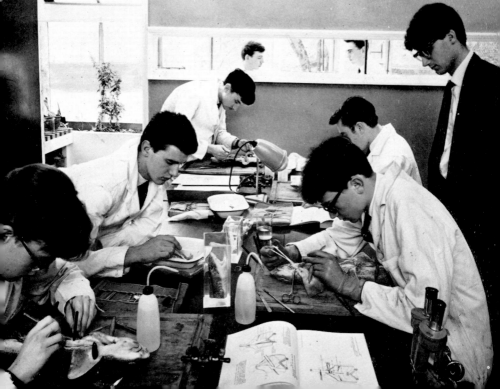

Dinner at School

Years ago children went home for their dinner, because mothers didnot go to work. They stayed at home to have their dinner for two hours. Then after the War mothers started to go to work in big modern factories. There was more money and more business, so more women were at work. Children couldnot go home because mothers were out at work. So they had school dinners. Now most modern schools have their own kitchens. Some big schools have to supply small schools. The school I go to is small so another school supplys us. In my school girls are trained to carry dinners to the infants. Girls are very good in the dinner hour. They help to set the table and cutlery. Lots of children come out for seconds. We have lots of helpers to give out the dinner like Mrs Lambert and Mrs Malin.

Christopher Thompson
Age 9

SCHOOL MEALS   *Left* A child at Gateforth Primary School, 1964, explains the theory and practice of school meals.   *Bottom left* Children at the Gateway Primary School, 1963, sitting down to 'family service', six to a table.

PRACTICAL ARITHMETIC   New approaches to number teaching – many of them as old as the London School Board – involve the children in measuring and weighing everyday objects as here at Normand Park School, 1962.

COMPREHENSIVE SCHOOLS Early designs like Kidbrooke, 1954, produced massive buildings for 1,800–2,000 pupils. Later, smaller schools were planned and more attention was paid in the design to breaking the large school down into smaller units.

Morning assembly at Archway School, 1965.

Nature Table
Monitor

"Peggy Ann Bowen"

acorns

hawthorn

Left A typical primary-school scene – the nature table at Danebury Primary School, 1959.   *Bottom left* Shallow learner-pools like this at Middle Row Primary School, 1969, give all children the chance to learn to swim.

Concentrated activity in craft work at Stockwell Primary School, 1967.

Domestic science gets a wider treatment to include all the interests which arise from family responsibilities and home-making.
Top right Supermarket skills at Hammersmith County School for Girls, 1968.
Bottom right Girls on a commercial course at the South Eastern College of Further Education, 1969, learn to use modern office equipment.

Working in the school flat at Tollington Park, 1963.

Lord Boyle, then
Parliamentary Secretary
at the Ministry of
Education, with children
at the Franklin D.
Roosevelt School for
physically handicapped
children, 1957.

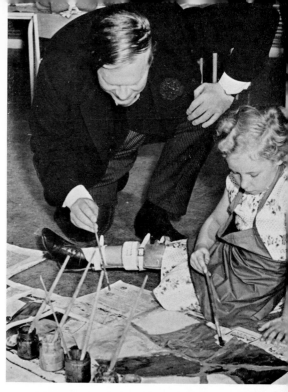

Using powerful
amplifying equipment to
teach deaf boys and girls
at the Oak Lodge Special
School, 1969.

Drama and music bring a response from children at Wycliffe Special School (educationally subnormal), 1969.

Northern Polytechnic is one of the colleges which have shared in the expansion of advanced work in technology.

EDUCATIONAL TELEVISION A primary school teacher presents a programme at the formal opening of the I.L.E.A. educational TV studios in Islington. By 1970 all London schools had been brought into the closed circuit network, and the new educational television centre had been set up in Battersea. Programmes are prepared and presented by practising London teachers on secondment, with the assistance of professional television staff.

what children do and what they achieve should be carefully and individually recorded.

Typical of the schools as a whole was the mixture of methods and the freedom with which heads chose their own combination of formal and progressive practice. A 'changed relationship' was noted 'between children and staff which is not confined to the progressive schools. Children are treated in most schools with greater respect and courtesy. . . . Discipline is largely a matter of personal relationship.'

How far a school was likely to go in introducing modern methods depended on the social environment as well as on the temperament and talents of the teachers. The tussle between larger, vaguer educational aims continued, especially in middle-class areas where parents remained obstinately concerned with 'traditional standards of arithmetic, English composition, grammar and spelling'. On the teaching of reading – again as in 1900,* said to be by 'look and say' and phonic methods 'in flexible combination' – the evidence had little to say, though the literacy survey at the end of the 1960s showed that alarmingly few teachers had been given specific instruction in how to teach reading, or any extensive introduction to the pedagogic theory behind different methods. When the survey appeared plans were hurried forward for more in-service training in the teaching of reading.

Once the traditional attachment to class teaching by age groups was weakened schools began to experiment with 'vertical grouping' – meaning, at the infant stage, teaching in 'family groups' containing 5- and 6-year-olds together, letting the strong help the weak and enabling each to go ahead at an individual pace. Enterprising junior school heads found virtue in extending the infant school methods upwards into the junior school.

Streaming – the division of year-groups into homogeneous teaching units on the basis of ability – came to be in question in more and more schools, for two different sets of reasons. First, streaming conflicted with ideas of equality; those who attacked streaming did so because they said it was a self-fulfilling prophecy which, by imposing a hierarchy on children, led them to conform to the premature assessments of their teachers. Second, it conflicted with the new organization of vertical grouping which was desired for other reasons.

After all, vertical grouping of its nature implied a wide spread of operational ability within a normal teaching group. Teachers who were

* See p. 48.

prepared to countenance this because they believed that it enabled individuals of different ages and abilities to help each other in many practical ways, were unlikely to see any overriding need to stream children into homogeneous year-groups. By 1964, un-streaming was still very much a minority phenomenon at the top of the junior school, but it was one which was spreading fairly rapidly by the end of the 1960s.

The essence of the new approach was a movement away from formal class-teaching to individual work and work in small groups. With this went a new attitude towards the organization of the school day – a much more flexible timetable – and to the division of school work into 'subjects'. Alongside these changes in organization and method, it was possible to point to more conventional innovations like the attempt to replace arid and mechanical teaching of arithmetic by a genuine introduction to mathematical concepts through the use of new teaching materials and new syllabuses developed by bodies such as the Schools Council and the Nuffield Foundation. Primary school science – Huxley's aim in the 1870s – had begun to make its way in the junior school with specially trained teachers and the use of up-to-date visual and aural aids.

Some of the most encouraging results were thought to have been obtained in English and particularly free writing and expression work, including the writing of poetry. This seemed to express much of the aims of the new methods – the release of the inner resources of the children and the search for ways of enabling them to capitalize on their own organized and unorganized experience. According to Sir Cyril Burt's sample testing of London children's writing, this had raised the level of interest and originality in the written work, but at the expense of the more mundane qualities of grammatical accuracy. In theory at least, the aims of creativity and operational efficiency were complementary, not conflicting; in practice, some schools were more successful at holding the ring than others.

How did the new methods spread from school to school in a system which leaves so much control of curriculum and method to the teaching staff? The L.C.C. and later I.L.E.A. inspectorate (including Mr Richard Palmer, staff inspector for primary education till his retirement in 1970) played an important part. So, too, of course, did the colleges of education where the philosophy of new primary methods was instilled into new generations of teachers in training. But in London it is also possible to point to particular schools where innovating heads showed what could be done and trained others in new techniques. Eliot Bank school at Lewisham was one example, where Miss A. D. Smith was not only an exponent of child-centred education herself, but had the gift of training, inspiring and encouraging her deputy heads to add their own original contribution. One of these was Mr Holliday Evans, who moved on to become head of Heathbrook school, Battersea, where he transformed the educational landscape with the aid of a young and enthusiastic staff. Others, like Miss Sheila Lane at Tidemill Junior School in Deptford, took a school in an educational priority area and, by dint of sheer inspiration and hard work, raised the quality of the educational offering which the children received, especially in the vital field of the English language – written and read, spoken and acted.

People like this were infectious examples. They trained teachers like themselves on their own staffs and through in-service courses and conferences they were influential on a wider scale. The L.C.C. backed them up in various ways. New methods demanded different furniture, more books, more and more imaginative equipment. New furniture was specially designed for the age groups for whom it was to be provided. Special storage units have been made to enable space to be better used. Cloakroom space has been saved by introducing trolleys for hats, coats and shoes which can be wheeled out of the way. School design reflected the new approach proving that better, more functional buildings could provide more teaching space at lower cost. Two experimental schools were built, the Vittoria school, Islington, and the Evelyn Lowe school at Camberwell.

The aim has been to group the teaching spaces in the most flexible way possible, combining a general teaching space, store cupboards, small group and individual work spaces and a quiet area, and to associate outdoor spaces with those indoors so that, in good weather, the flexibility can be increased still more. By using a very open plan, with mobile screen trolleys, teaching spaces can be combined in an almost unlimited number of ways for story-telling or group-work or practical activities.

Evelyn Lowe school, designed by the Architects and Buildings Branch at the Department of Education and Science, was experimental in the sense that it carried these ideas further than they were being taken in other primary schools; but the ideas themselves were not new. They derived directly from the new teaching methods and even in the old and often sturdily intractable buildings attempts were being made, by knocking down walls and pushing out bays, to make such modification as could be afforded under the minor works programmes to give effect to these same ideas.

The main planning principle, adopted in many of the later designs, was to try to plan for pairs of class rooms, with their own related 'resource areas'. Mr Palmer devised his own ingenious pattern of two class rooms with swivelling walls which presented an inexpensive method of offering thirty-six alternative ways in which a given area could be divided.

13 *Immigrants and priority areas*

Partly as a result of the recommendations of the Plowden Committee, partly as a result of the urban programme which was prompted by growing concern about coloured immigration, London has been able during the later 1960s to concentrate additional physical and human resources in the schools with the most difficult jobs to do.

The Plowden Report introduced the idea of 'positive discrimination' and suggested that areas where the social and educational circumstances were least good should receive extra help in the form of buildings, equipment, apparatus and books, ancillary and teaching staff and so on. In practice, the concept of the priority area was replaced by that of the priority school, and the programmes for educational priority merged into larger programmes of urban aid, in an attempt specially to assist areas where immigrants were numerous without appearing to discriminate in their favour.

London first became aware of an immigrant 'problem' in the mid-1950s. Traditionally, London had been a cosmopolitan city with particular localities and schools with immigrant populations. But in 1956 when Dr H. A. T. Child, the L.C.C. educational psychologist, reported on the primary education of immigrants, the 'problem' was still being played down. At this time, the Cypriots were the largest immigrant contingent (1,480), followed by the Indians and Pakistanis (632), Poles (522), Italians (410) and West Indians (351). Then, as in every subsequent report, the main educational problem was seen in terms of language, and particularly the basic difficulties of those who arrived at school unable to speak, let alone read, English. Later, as the West Indians took over the lead as the largest single group, more came to be understood about their linguistic needs which could be camouflaged by the superficial similarities between standard English and plantation English (not to mention the added confusions of the Cockney tongue).

By the time the I.L.E.A. gave evidence to the House of Commons

Select Committee on Race Relations, the figures (1968) had sharply risen. The total of 5,500 in 1956 had gone up to 62,000. The West Indians had become the biggest single group, numbering 34,500. Greek and Turkish Cypriots (8,500) and Indians and Pakistanis (6,000) took second and third place.

London considered and rejected the advice of the Department of Education and Science which was to disperse immigrants by 'bussing' them from areas of high concentration to schools where the proportion of immigrants was low. In London it was felt that, at the primary level, the most important consideration was the personal security of the immigrant child who had enough to tackle in settling down in a new and strange home without being transported to a school some miles away from his own circle of potential friends.

In the primary schools, the immigrant language problems have been met, for the most part, by extra staffing, aimed at enabling small groups of non-English speakers to be given special help without removing them from the school community. At the secondary level, where late arrivals in the country half-way through their schooling present much greater difficulties, some nine special centres have been set up for intensive language tuition. The children normally divide their time between school and centre. Some schools have their own units. The advantage of the centres is that they enable expert teachers of English as a second language to make the most contribution for those whose need is greatest. The centres have to be large enough to justify a full team.

Their work is backed up in the schools where the percentage of immigrants is high by teachers who receive short in-service training courses. Each summer, the I.L.E.A. holds a special induction course for new entrants to the London teaching service to acquaint them with the immigrants' educational needs, and a one-term course is offered each year for fifteen teachers wishing to specialize in English as a second language. At the primary level, a survey carried out in 1967 showed that, as might be expected, the educational standards achieved by pupils from overseas were directly related to the length of time they had been in England and attended London schools. There were also differences between various groups, according to their country of origin, which suggested that the West Indians had more difficulties than others, possibly because of their linguistic background. Because of their learning difficulties, immigrants – particularly West Indians – have begun to take up a disproportionately large number of places in schools for the educationally subnormal. By 1967, they accounted for twenty-eight per cent of the educationally subnormal places, although immigrants only represented fifteen per cent of the pupils in the ordinary schools. This gave rise to a good deal of concern – including accusations of prejudice and discrimination. In functional terms, these children corresponded to the official definition of educationally subnormal, although the reasons for their failure to learn might in many cases be different from those of the native-born London children.

With new language tuition and special basic education units for those whose backwardness is due to the interruption of schooling or prolonged absence at some earlier stage, the I.L.E.A. hope to change this. But in many cases, failure to learn, for whatever cause, has produced behaviour problems, and without suitable special arrangements in small classes it is not always possible to do better for the individual pupil than to send him to a sympathetic special school.

Most – but not all – of the educational priority schemes have included measures which have had a bearing on immigrant needs. London has gone further than most authorities to follow the Plowden suggestion and establish priorities based on a set of social and educational criteria not unlike those which, back in 1885,* had been used as the basis of the extra payments for teachers in schools of special difficulty. Schools have been ranked in order of priority according to objective criteria. Extra teachers and non-teaching staff have been allocated to the first fifty priority schools on the list. The first 100 schools have had their capitation allowance for books and equipment increased by 5s. a pupil. Teachers in the first seventy-eight schools on the list have qualified for the special £75 a year E.P.A. allowance.

These schools have also benefited from the I.L.E.A.'s two-year £2¼ million building programme for E.P.A. projects approved in 1968 – £1½ million for twenty new schools and major remodelling projects, and the rest in sums of up to £25,000 to make improvements in other old schools. Further instalments of the urban programme have extended the building grants to other schools when the proportion of immigrants has topped thirty per cent.

* Some of the schools qualifying for extra support in 1970 are the same as those which benefited under the 1885 scheme.

The following are the criteria which have been used:

Criterion	Measure	Source
1. Social class composition	Percentage of males in unskilled and semi-skilled occupations	1966 Census
2. Large families	Percentage of children in households of six or more persons	1966 Census
3. Overcrowding	Percentage of households living at density of more than $1\frac{1}{2}$ persons per room	1966 Census
4. Housing stress	Percentage of households without inside WC	1966 Census
5. Cash supplements	Percentage of pupils receiving free meals	1966 September return
6. Absenteeism	Percentage absent during first week in May	1967 May return
7. Immigrants	Percentage of immigrants in school	Form 7(i), 1967
8. Handicapped pupils	Percentage of pupils in bottom (lowest twenty-five per cent) ability groups	1967 Transfer
9. Teacher turn-over	Percentage of teachers in school less than 3 years	1967 Teacher record card
10. Pupil turn-over	Percentage of pupils who moved during year	1965/6 attendance card

The following table gives an idea how the priority schools compare with the national average:

	1	2	3	4	5	6	7	8	9	10
1st school	47·8	43·4	15·9	35·6	29·5	14·7	68·1	75·0	83·3	55·5
50th school	42·1	39·1	10·7	30·4	24·3	12·3	53·0	65·0	71·4	39·1
100th school	39·3	36·6	9·1	26·2	13·5	10·8	35·0	49·4	66·7	28·5
150th school	32·7	33·2	5·4	22·2	11·4	9·5	21·8	38·9	57·1	23·5
England and Wales average	22·7[1]	20·6	1·2	19·8	5·1	8·4[2]	2·5	25·0	35·6[3]	9·5[1]

1. National figures abstracted from 1961 Census.
2. I.L.E.A. average (1967).
3. Not strictly comparable; figures used for England and Wales abstracted from Plowden.

14 *Going comprehensive*

The 1944 Act demanded one reform of overriding importance. Elementary education was to be swept away. Instead, the educational span was divided into two successive stages, primary and secondary. In social terms this meant two things. The abolition of the elementary school implied the ending of the class-based system of basic schooling from 5 to 14, tailored to the supposed needs of the working-class child. The corollary to this was a redefinition of secondary education which, in theory at least, stripped it of its special middle-class, grammar school meaning. For countless Londoners, 'secondary school' would no doubt continue to mean 'grammar school' for many years to come, just as many would still talk about the elementary school to mean the primary school. But the 1944 Act was making a change of fundamental importance, and the next twenty-five years were to be spent trying to carry it out.

While the London school plan was being drawn up on comprehensive principles, it was recognized that the problems of school reorganization would not wait for the long-term resources which would be needed to carry it out. In 1946, London still had 174 all-age elementary schools: most of the council schools had been divided into senior and junior schools on Hadow lines between 1924 and 1939, and almost all the remainder were reorganized in existing buildings on the return from evacuation. A number of Church all-age schools, however, remained, and had to wait for building programmes.

The first step, then, was to turn the senior schools into secondary schools – changes of name which were backed up, more or less according to circumstances, by changes in staffing and supplies, and, in the course of time, by the addition of workshops and practical rooms. The L.C.C. was under no illusion that this was more than a temporary stage in a move towards a more ambitious and generous view of secondary education. But at first the pressure of numbers was in the primary schools; it was there that new building had to be concentrated, and the huge plans for custom-built comprehensives inevitably had to wait.

The junior technical and art schools, of which London was inordinately proud, were separated from the senior institutes, of which till then they had been a part. In time they, too, were to be absorbed in the comprehensive schools, but in the meantime they were reorganized as secondary schools alongside grammar and modern schools, and the age of admission was brought down from 13 to 11.

As for the county and aided grammar schools, they too were transformed by the Education Act. Superficially they remained the same, their curriculum little modified by the change in their main examinations from School and Higher School Certificate to G.C.E. at O- and A-level. But the 1944 Act changed them profoundly by abolishing fees. The abolition of fees meant the abolition also of the fee-payer, and selection for the grammar schools for all pupils on the basis of the 11 plus.

The grammar school fee-payer had long been an anomaly. Between the wars there had been plenty of people ready to point out the logical absurdity of limiting the number of scholarships awarded, when it cost the L.C.C. more in subsidies to support a fee-payer at a grammar school than a pupil at one of the free selective central schools. Moreover, it had traditionally been the fee-payers who tended to leave early and had to be cajoled into staying on by commercial courses. An end to fee-paying paved the way for a rise in standards at the grammar school and coincided also with the decline in early leaving noticeable from the 1950s onwards which gave the grammar schools (or many of them) the stronger sixth forms which they soon came to believe they had always had.

In addition to providing grammar school places at county and voluntary schools, the L.C.C. also took up free places at a number of independent and direct-grant schools – notably Dulwich, which remained an independent school while allocating a majority of places to London pupils. The number of places was reduced when the population trends and the increase of academic places in L.C.C. schools reduced the need. In 1969, the I.L.E.A. made the 'free' places at the independent schools into 'assisted' places, which meant that the parents of new entrants were, thereafter, required to contribute towards the fees on an income scale.

It is perhaps inevitable that most of the attention should be centred on the development of comprehensive schools. This might give a distorted view if it obscured the continued importance of the London grammar schools and their high prestige throughout the quarter of a century which followed the 1944 Act. Some schools enjoyed more esteem than others. Some had new buildings; others soldiered on in old. But they retained a strong position, continuing to take around 17–20 per cent of the entry into all London secondary schools, and they continued to provide the larger proportion of all London pupils who were entered for G.C.E. examinations.

The L.C.C. attitude to these schools for much of this period was inevitably ambivalent. The voluntary grammar schools included some schools in the very first class, of which education committee members – including those who were most zealously behind the comprehensive scheme – were naturally proud. Yet the aided schools* represented a thorn in the flesh to the comprehensive schools, preventing many of them from receiving a balanced intake and, by their continued existence, forcing the authority into compromise and inconsistency. Throughout the period, from first to last, the comprehensive controversy remained near the surface of the political debate, complicating the lives of heads, and inspectors and educational administrators, and making it difficult to produce background papers on the development of comprehensive schools without these being used by protagonists of either view as if they were political tracts.

Savage and Brown were agreed on one thing. In the London context, with a flourishing range of grammar schools already in the field, the comprehensive schools needed to be protected from their over-eager friends. They were both opposed to attempts to start up in makeshift accommodation, wanting to make the new purpose-built schools which would appear in the mid-1950s the show-cases for the experiment.

To gain experience of comprehensive organization, however, eight experimental comprehensive schools were set up between 1946 and 1949 by amalgamating schools in existing buildings. These became the nucleus of some of the comprehensive schools developed during the 1950s. Some of them in the experimental period were very much more successful than others. Some had cards heavily stacked against them, with divided buildings and difficult social backgrounds. A notable success against the odds was at Walworth where a brilliant headmistress, Miss O'Reilly, proved how much could be done under conditions which were anything but easy.

The schools were not 'fully comprehensive', a term the L.C.C. began to use to distinguish one comprehensive school from another, when the splendidly vague term 'large secondary school' ceased to suffice. But, according to the education officer's report,

---

* Some of the aided schools like St Olave's, Bermondsey, moved out of the London area, thus removing themselves from the consequences of London's comprehensive plans.

... three points seem to be firmly established as a result of the experience gained in these schools:

1. The less able pupils benefited educationally and socially.
2. A number of pupils who would not normally have had the opportunity of taking the examination for the General Certificate of Education have done so very successfully.
3. A number of pupils who would normally have left school at 15 have stayed on longer.

Many of these schools – and others later – were much smaller than the model for the fully comprehensive school laid down in the London plan. These were the schools which started out as 'county complements' – intended to be developed in association with aided grammar schools in those areas where nothing could prevent the comprehensive school from being heavily 'creamed'. As things turned out, this form of association failed to work and it was decided to develop the former 'county complements' as 'large secondary schools' with the aim of allowing them in time to grow into fully comprehensive schools. At any time there is room for argument about what, in a mixed system, constitutes a fully comprehensive school, but it was not disputed that some of these would take a fair time to develop.

One division which can be made among the comprehensive schools developed in the 1950s and 1960s is between those which were expanded from existing grammar schools (like Mayfield school, Putney) and those which were based on the amalgamation of senior and central schools. Without exception, for reasons which are not hard to appreciate, the ex-grammar schools had a head start, inheriting a tradition and a sixth form which otherwise took some years to acquire. This had to be recognized and accepted: the background of every school was different, each fitted into a different social milieu, each differed in popularity and standing with parents. In some places comprehensive schools ranged themselves in a definite pecking order. Comparisons between such sharply differentiated institutions were liable to be dangerous and invidious; generalization about them was almost certain to be misleading.*

---

* The title 'comprehensive school' covered from time to time institutions as widely different as Michael Duane's Risinghill, and Rhodes Boyson's Highbury Grove. One side of the story of Duane's attempt to run a comprehensive school on progressive lines, and of the circumstances in which Risinghill was closed, has been told in a brilliantly partisan book by Mrs Leila Berg. A series of clashes between Duane and the I.L.E.A. administration over the way in which the school was run raised burning controversy about corporal punishment, a head's relationship with his staff and with the inspectorate, and the real and imaginary reasons why the school premises were put to other use.

The first of the custom-built comprehensives to open was Kidbrooke, with thirteen forms of entry, a girls' school at Eltham. It was here that Miss Florence Horsbrugh, the Minister of Education, put a spoke in London's wheel by refusing to allow the incorporation of Eltham Hill School, a girls' grammar school, in the new comprehensive. This was a direct challenge, made worse by circumstances which laid Miss Horsbrugh open to the charge that she had herself stirred up some of the opposition from parents which she had later, in a quasi-judicial capacity, judged to be grounds for stopping the scheme.

In time, the proportion of 'academic' pupils applying to Kidbrooke built up so that, when the L.C.C. inspectorate prepared a full report on the progress of the comprehensive schools in 1961, Kidbrooke could be included among those which had become 'fully comprehensive'. This meant that, in the opinion of the inspectors, the school was getting a reasonably balanced intake. No selection exam was, of course, used to pick pupils for comprehensive schools, but the continued existence of a range of grammar schools made it necessary to retain a form of individual evaluation by the primary schools. From 1965 onwards this depended on the use of primary school records and teachers' estimates to prepare profiles of primary school leavers which could be scaled against objective tests. This meant that individual children were not examined in any formal 11 plus examination, but the secondary schools could be provided with teachers' estimates in a reasonably comparable form.

Selection for grammar schools for those who continued to choose them was based on these primary profiles. They were also used as the basis of a system of banding designed to ensure that all 'fully comprehensive' schools had a share of children from the upper, middle and lower ability ranges. Details of the scheme were modified towards the end of the period after difficulties had arisen in the middle 1960s as the intake into secondary schools declined for demographic reasons. This had the incidental effect of stepping up the proportion of the age group who were offered grammar school places, causing chagrin to the comprehensive school heads. Meanwhile, the number of comprehensive schools also increased, making it harder to maintain the informal distinction between 'fully comprehensive' schools and the rest, and, hence, giving rise to complaints from the better established comprehensive schools that the butter was being spread more thinly.

In October 1961, the L.C.C. published a report on the working of the comprehensive schools based on a series of inquiries undertaken by the inspectorate. The glare of publicity meant that the authority had been under constant pressure from admirers and critics alike to publish 'results' achieved by the comprehensive schools which might then be used as grist for the mills of controversy. This there was a natural reluctance to do. The 1961 report, like the 1966 report which followed in its turn, was an attempt to counter the demands of those who wished to pull the plant up by the roots to see how well it was growing. It took the form of an interim survey which covered sixteen selected and 'representative' comprehensives.

By 1961, London had fifty-nine comprehensive schools in all taking 53.4 per cent of the secondary school population. These schools included twenty-two in new purpose-built buildings, and the remainder in former senior and central schools. There were twenty-one county grammar schools still operating as separate selective schools and five technical schools continued to take in a selected entry at 11. Only forty-one county schools were classified as secondary modern: where an unselective school was being built up into a comprehensive school it was placed in a separate category of 'other' schools of which there were fifty.

Of the sixteen schools in the survey, nine were described as 'fully comprehensive' and one, Bowbrook, was an intended county complement which, with only a five-form entry, had not yet reached the degree of comprehensiveness to be returned as a comprehensive school on the Ministry of Education Form 7. Only two schools, Parliament Hill and Wandsworth, were based on former grammar schools. Three were developed from the first experimental comprehensive schools started at the end of the 1940s.

The inspectorate had deliberately chosen schools which differed widely to show the variety of circumstances which had to be faced and the variety of resources available. They were, therefore, most reluctant to draw general conclusions. They described the organization of the schools and their curriculum and how individual schools might develop particular 'special studies' – that is to say, practical and vocational subjects. For example, Walworth's special studies included commerce and engineering; Kidbrooke's included millinery, catering, dressmaking and tailoring.

A continuing topic of interest was the way in which large schools broke up into smaller units in order to present the pupil with smaller communities within the large community of the whole unit. Two main methods were described: vertical grouping, by houses; and horizontal grouping, by years. These patterns were superimposed on the normal social divisions of forms and sets. The vertical and horizontal organization provided ways of integrating children into mixed ability groups and were held to be important in relation to the larger social aims of the school, as well as to the individual welfare of the children. (Later and disputed findings by a London School of Economics sociologist, Miss Julienne Ford,* cast some doubt on the efficacy of the house system as a means of social integration: according to her survey, the children's individual social relationships were not based on the house group.) But, for all that, the house system had an organizational value apart from its potential as a social solvent, in that it provided units of administration of a more manageable size within the large school.

Much of the public debate continued to centre on comparisons of the effectiveness of different forms of secondary organization as they affected the most intelligent pupils – those who would otherwise be in grammar schools. The 1961 survey discussed the academic work of the schools at length, describing the growth of the sixth forms at some of the new schools. A few comprehensive schools, like Forest Hill, began to organize fast streams, to enable the most able pupils to take some O-level subjects at the end of the fourth year. A feature of the schools was the wide variety of options open to the pupils, given the resources which could be mobilized by very large schools. In all cases the progress of the schools was influenced by the degree of 'creaming' from neighbouring grammar schools: where an existing grammar school was the nucleus of the comprehensive school the paper results were much better, though it was properly emphasized that these examination results could not necessarily be taken as a sure guide to the true merit of the schools without more information about the children who entered them and their social circumstances. More often than not this was not appreciated; the tendentious association of the idea of 'excellence' with the education of clever pupils continued to obscure the discussion. The 1961 survey was at pains to show that the comprehensive school aimed at excellence for all the pupils, and that excellent remedial teaching was as important a feature of these schoools as good academic results.

Five years later the Inner London Education Authority received a second survey carried out by the inspectorate. It took the form of a report by the deputy education officer, Dr Eric Briault, and the chief inspector, Dr L. W. Payling, which appeared in March 1967, and was somewhat over-

* *Social Class and the Comprehensive School,* Julienne Ford, 1969.

shadowed by the electioneering which preceded the 1967 London land-slide elections when political control changed for the first time since 1934.

By the time this (1966) report was prepared there were seventy-seven comprehensive schools and the first batch of custom-built comprehensives had been open for not more than twelve years. All the schools offered O- and A-levels; twenty-nine were mixed schools, twenty-five were for boys only and twenty-three were for girls; all had provision for 'special courses' of a technical or commercial kind. The comprehensive schools were still operating in the shadow of the grammar school which took in some 18·8 per cent of the entry at 11.

One of the matters on which the survey sought to shed some light was the success of the comprehensive school with those who had not been judged to be of 'grammar school' ability at 11. Figures were quoted from eleven schools with a sixth-form population of 547, none of whom had 'passed the 11 plus' – the report used a more elegant London euphemism – and for thirty-five non-grammar schools with 1,020 pupils in the seventh and eighth year, seventy per cent of whom were also late developers, mostly on A-level courses.

As one measure of the achievement of the comprehensive schools, the survey showed that in 1960 the London comprehensives admitted 1,648 'grammar pupils' but that, five years later, some 7,613 pupils passed O-levels in at least one subject. These figures were not conclusive proof of anything – except the examination performance of individuals – but the willingness to publish them marked a certain stage in the developing confidence of the comprehensive school heads and of the I.L.E.A. administrators.

A major social change which had begun to affect secondary schools everywhere was the tendency to stay at school beyond the minimum school-leaving age. This was the subject of comment in the education officer's report on the three years from 1954 to 1957, when he noted that the percentage of pupils of 15 and 16 in all types of London schools had risen as follows:

Year	15+	16+
1952	34	12·9
1954	37·2	13·9
1956	38·3	16·0
1957	42·2	17·5

In the education officer's report for 1957–62 the trend in London county secondary schools had continued:

Year	15+	16+	17+	18+	19+
1958	44·6	20·0	7·2	2·5	0·4
1959	46·6	21·9	8·2	2·8	0·4
1960	48·3	22·4	9·1	3·1	0·4
1961	48·5	23·9	9·7	3·4	0·5
1962	50·0	24·7	11·2	3·8	0·5

In common with the rest of Southern England, London reflected this trend with better than average figures. No one could establish a causal relationship between comprehensive schools and staying on, but what the 1966 survey did was to compare the staying-on rate for 'non-grammar' pupils in London comprehensives with the national staying-on rate in non-grammar schools. The result showed the London schools in a highly favourable light:

	Percentage staying on to		
	15+	16+	17+
All non-grammar schools (January 1964)	48·7	10·5	2·9
Non-grammar pupils in London comprehensive schools (January 1964)	64·7	23·0	7·6

This tendency to stay on was seen in the growth of the sixth forms and in particular in the growth of the number of 'new' sixth-formers to which the 1966 report devoted some attention – the new group of pupils in the sixth year who were not engaged in post-O-level courses, but many of whom were taking O-levels in the sixth form, or who were on general courses.

These swelled the numbers of sixth-formers, and their success was a source of pride for the comprehensive schools, but their teaching needs were not the same as those of the pupils of the 'old' orthodox sixth form. One of the continuing causes for concern was the small size of the 'academic' sixth forms in many comprehensive schools, and the consequently extravagant demands on staff if a wide range of sixth-form options were to be offered.

This was more especially a problem for the smaller comprehensive schools – those with five and six forms of entry. In May 1967 a working group was set up to study this aspect of comprehensive school organization and came up, eighteen months later, with some startling facts.

In the first place, they showed that, while the number of post-O-level pupils in London's non-grammar schools had declined from about 6,150 in 1964 to 5,600 in 1968, the number of 'new' sixth-formers had jumped from 162 to 2,344. The decline in the academic sixth form was demographic, and was consistent with a slightly rising proportion of the smaller age group entering the grammar schools. The percentage of pupils entering both the academic and non-academic sixth forms had risen – from 10·6 and 7·9 per cent respectively in 1964, to 15·8 and 12·4 per cent in 1968.

What emerged about the distribution of the sixth-form pupils only served to underline the links between the neighbourhoods which the schools served and their educational character. Only fifty-three of the 208 schools with sixth forms had more than 100 pupils, 'academic' or 'non-academic', in their sixth-form group.

The exercise turned into a statistical puzzle – how, with the number of pupils available, academic and non-academic, divided between first-, second- and third-year groups, and various subjects of study, could the teaching be organized in groups of economic and efficient size?

The consensus of opinion canvassed by the working group concluded that sixth forms ought to be able to offer at least ten to twelve A-level subjects, and that there should be generally not less than five pupils in a sixth-form teaching group. This demanded an academic year-group of at least forty, if the sixth-form pupil–teacher ratio were not to fall below 11·3 : 1.

On this basis, a number of comprehensive schools and grammar schools could be deemed to have sixth forms which were not 'viable' – the working party's term – and various remedies, such as combined sixth forms or cooperation with colleges of further education, were mooted. It is obvious that the question of the viable comprehensive sixth form in London is in large measure that of the continued existence of the separate grammar school.

Circular 10/65, in which Mr Anthony Crosland requested local education authorities to submit comprehensive plans, produced a scheme from the Labour-controlled I.L.E.A., shortly before the 1967 elections, which promised a speeding up of the reorganization process, with the creation of more comprehensive schools (using old and separated buildings where necessary) so that by 1970 the number of all-in schools would have gone up from seventy-eight to 111, and the number of grammar schools would have shrunk from seventy-one to forty-nine.

The Conservatives immediately withdrew the plan after taking over political control, and the new leader of the education committee of the I.L.E.A., Mr Christopher Chataway, spent an arduous six months devising and negotiating a compromise scheme which, while providing for some progress towards the comprehensive ideal, satisfied his back-bench supporters that grammar schools would also continue. By 1970, the number of comprehensives had risen to eighty-five.

Two events in 1970 changed the outlook for London's secondary education – Labour won back control of I.L.E.A. at the London elections while losing the general election. The incoming Labour group led by Mr Ashley Bramall immediately signified their intention to speed up the comprehensive plan. But whereas Labour had intended to legislate at Westminster to compel authorities to go comprehensive, and might have helped London deal with the aided grammar schools, a Conservative Secretary of State is inclined to defend existing grammar schools.

London's secondary education plans for the 1970s are, therefore, in the melting pot as the last decade of the first century of public education draws to a close. Whatever happens something will be required sooner or later to resolve the contradictions of a mixed economy of selective and allegedly comprehensive schools existing side by side – a contradiction in terms which can only be defended as a half-way house to some more rational system.

15 Further and higher education

No part of the system has shown more dramatic growth than further education – not only in numbers, but in the level of work. Neat comparisons are obscured by changes in what has constituted this particular section of the educational front: the cutting off of the junior technical schools (to become part of secondary) reduced the amount of full-time work coming under this heading. But the rapid expansion of full-time work at the post-school age and particularly of advanced work in higher technological education has altered the picture beyond recognition.

In all this, the most important stimulus has been the generous provision of student grants – the permissive powers of the 1944 Act being strengthened by later legislation. The readiness to pay fees and maintenance grants (against a means test) for students in a wide range of university, college of education and further education courses has powered this expansion of numbers in a way nothing else could have done. The result has been a transformation of the further education scene. By 1970, grants were being made to 18,000 students in further and higher education at a cost of £6·3 million.

By 1945 London already had a further education system that was complex and comprehensive. Progress in the previous forty years had in some ways been as remarkable as the more publicized progress of the twenty years that followed. The annual cost of further education in the London County Council area in 1948 was almost £3 million compared with less than £400,000 spent by the T.E.B. in 1904, much of it on secondary education. The grants made by the Council to the aided polytechnics had increased in the same forty years from just over £48,000 to £820,000.

In 1947 London had a population of 3,402,400. 108,000 were between the ages of 15 and 18. Just over 13,000 of this age group were still attending secondary schools, and another 2,500 were attending full-time courses at further education colleges. Within the county there were thirty polytechnics and technical colleges, thirteen art schools and departments, twenty-one colleges or departments of commerce – of which only six offered full-time courses. In addition, part-time vocational education was provided in twenty-seven commercial and technical institutes, mainly for young people, and non-vocational part-time evening education in thirteen literary institutes, fifteen men's evening institutes, thirty evening institutes for women and twenty-one recreational institutes for young people. There were also two general institutes at Forest Hill and Sydenham. Finally the L.C.C. maintained eight day continuation colleges at Brixton, the City, Hammersmith, Islington, Kingsway, Lewisham, Hackney and Woolwich.

The main lines of the scheme of polytechnics, technical, commercial and art colleges remained those laid down in 1909 and, for the evening institutes, in 1913. Section 42 of the 1944 Education Act gave the Minister power to ask L.E.A.s to draw up schemes for further education – including, of course, provision for the county colleges which were intended to provide further education on a day release basis for all young people between 15 and 18 who were not in some other form of full-time education. In March 1947, Circular 133 went out to all L.E.A.s requiring them to draw up a scheme within twelve months. After some delays London's plan was sent to the Minister in 1949.

That scheme is still the basis of the Inner London Education Authority's plans for the development of further education although it has been extensively modified since and a comprehensive review took place after the publication in 1956 of Sir David Eccles's White Paper on technical education.

The L.C.C. estimated that the new county colleges which would replace the junior technical and commercial institutes and the day continuation colleges would have to take 85,000 students – aged between 16 and 18; it was assumed that makeshift arrangements would be able to deal with the 15-year-olds until the school-leaving age was raised. If each student were to be in the college for one whole day a week, the county colleges would have to provide about 17,000 places. Some thirty-four colleges were planned at an estimated capital cost of £14 million.

The proposal to bring back the ill-fated day continuation schools of a quarter of a century earlier in the shape of thirty-four county colleges was the most controversial part of the L.C.C.'s scheme for further education. When the plan was discussed first in November 1948, Sir Percy Harris, the veteran Liberal on the L.C.C., said he was 'appalled by the ambitious character of the plan for county colleges' and he appealed for a more modest scheme that would have a better chance of coming into operation. He repeated his opinion that county colleges were not an immediate possibility when the scheme was finally approved by the L.C.C. in March 1949. The events of the next twenty years showed that his fears were justified, county colleges never got off the ground – principally because the school-leaving age was not raised and any idea of making day release compulsory remained only the purest of good intentions. When London did finally set up the colleges of further education to serve the same kind of young people as the abortive county colleges had been intended to serve, they were closer to the modest scheme urged by Sir Percy in 1948 than the more ambitious county plan.

With the failure, for economic reasons, of the county college scheme went a continuing feature of further education in London as elsewhere – the explosive growth of vocational and technical further education, especially at technician and higher levels, while non-vocational and recreational further education made slower progress. In 1948 this emphasis on technical education was deliberate.

A considerable amount of high-level work, including degree courses, was going on in the aided polytechnics and colleges. In architecture, for instance, the Regent Street Polytechnic and the Northern Polytechnic were the main centres. Both ran full-time courses lasting five years and leading to the final examinations of the R.I.B.A. In both colleges parallel part-time courses which exempted students from the intermediate examination of the R.I.B.A. were offered. In 1949 there were some 18,000 students on various engineering courses and there were plans for this number to rise to 30,000. In a dynamic situation there was the constant pressure to 'rationalize' and 'concentrate' – two injunctions which seem like a refrain through the post-war expansion of advanced further education. The 1949 scheme recommended that engineering courses should be rationalized, and that advanced courses should be concentrated. Eight central colleges – Battersea, Borough, Regent Street, Northampton and Woolwich polytechnics, and South East London, Wandsworth, Westminster technical colleges – were to provide advanced courses for students from a wide area. Six other colleges were planned to run the lower-level engineering courses taking their students as far as possible from their own localities.

The 1949 proposals for engineering courses proved to be too ambitious, and only two colleges – Battersea and Northampton polytechnics – were able to shed all their lower-level work and concentrate entirely on advanced courses. In 1961 the plan was revised and the idea of 'central' and 'local' colleges for engineering was abandoned. Instead, engineering courses up to the level of the first year of O.N.C. were offered in ten colleges – now known as colleges of further education – and all other non-advanced courses were organized in seven area and three regional colleges. Two other regional colleges Woolwich Polytechnic and Sir John Cass College – together with the two C.A.T.s concentrated on advanced courses, with each college specializing in a particular field: Sir John Cass, for instance, in advanced courses in metallurgy.

A similar process of differentiation and concentration was planned for commercial education. The twenty-five centres for senior work were reduced to twelve, each with the capacity for 2,500 evening students. Six of them – Regent Street, City of London, Holborn, College for the Distributive Trades, Kennington and Westminster colleges of commerce – offered courses up to an advanced level in one or two specialized branches of commercial education. The other six colleges were designated as local colleges offering courses in all branches of commerce up to the level of intermediate professional examinations. Management education – which in 1945 was a comparatively insignificant branch of commercial education – was provided at Regent Street Polytechnic, which in the next twenty years was to establish a national reputation in this field, and at the City of London College.

In 1961 this arrangement was modified. Kennington lost its potential senior status, and two new colleges were added to the list – Balham and Tooting, now South West London College, and the West London College of Commerce – and departments of commerce at four polytechnics and technical colleges were also allowed to concentrate on work above the standard of O-level.

One of the peculiarities of London's further education system – dating back to the turn of the century – has been its large number of specialist technical colleges: Brixton School of Building, College for the Distributive Trades, Cordwainers' Technical College, Leathersellers' Technical College, London School of Printing and Graphic Arts, Shoreditch College for the Garment Trades, Smithfield College of Food Technology. The names have changed from time to time and colleges have been merged and re-formed, but London's industrial history is preserved in its technical colleges. The very size and diversity of the industries in London – nearly every industry except for mining, cotton and wool, and agriculture is represented in the county – had produced richness and variety, and nearly every major technical subject was taught in one or more London colleges. Two future universities, one university college, and five polytechnics – of the new 1966 White Paper variety – were to develop out of the polytechnics and colleges of London in 1949.

Throughout the twenty-five years since the end of the war, steady expansion of adult education has taken place – although not on the same scale as the expansion of technical education. By 1955–6, more than 105,000 students were attending the L.C.C. institutes – four per cent of the total population over school-leaving age. Before the war, the proportion had been only 3·3 per cent; by 1968–9 it had risen to 7·5 per cent of the total population over 15 – 189,000 students. As a result of the 1956 review the forty-five separate men's and women's institutes were abolished and replaced by thirty-three general mixed adult education institutes. In fact the distinction between the men's and women's institutes had become increasingly blurred over the previous ten years. By 1955 almost one out of every five students in 'men's' institutes were women and increasingly men had been allowed to take courses at 'women's' institutes. At the same time, the city's literary institutes were reorganized: two – South East and South West London – were closed, but the two central London literary institutes, City and St Marylebone, remained.

Each of the thirty-three institutes was to have about five branches, based mainly on local secondary schools, and arranged so that no one would have to be more than half a mile from a branch. Between 3,000 and 4,000 students was considered the ideal size for an institute. In fact, although two of the four literary institutes were abolished, much of their work was transferred to the new general institutes, and literature, languages and liberal arts were included along with crafts, cookery and physical education.

The Further and Higher Education Sub-committee of the I.L.E.A., in their evidence to the Russell Committee on Adult Education published early in 1970, mentioned some of the difficulties of providing a comprehensive system of adult education in London.

It is not often realised that London is an amalgam of a large number of villages and almost self-contained neighbourhood units which over the years have been absorbed geographically but not psychologically by the sprawling development of London. Each neighbourhood has its own idiosyncratic nature; if, for example, the local population is in the habit of looking traditionally to the west for its shopping centre or social recreation, it will not consider going *eastwards* or crossing a road or park not normally crossed, for leisure time activities. This is still an important and a very real factor in London.

G*

As well as its own adult education institutes, the L.C.C., and the I.L.E.A., its successor, continued to make grants to such institutions as the Royal School of Needlework, Morley College, Goldsmiths' College department for adult studies, and the Mary Ward Settlement. In 1969–70, grants to such colleges and institutes totalled £210,000.

A major review of London's technical and commercial education was carried out after the publication of the 1956 White Paper on technical education. Three London colleges were among the nine colleges of advanced technology which were set up after the White Paper – Chelsea Polytechnic, which, after the Robbins Report, was to become a constituent college of London University, Northampton Polytechnic, which was to become the City University, and Battersea Polytechnic which, was to become ten years later the University of Surrey at Guildford.

To a certain extent the decision on which of the nine London colleges which already had a high proportion of advanced work should be elevated to C.A.T. status had to be arbitrary. Full-time advanced work on a sandwich basis was one pointer to the future. Another was success in London external examinations. Yet another was the ambition of the governing body and the principal. By deciding to create the C.A.T.s, and cutting through the arguments which had held up advance in higher technological education for the previous ten years, Sir David Eccles, then Minister of Education, forced the L.C.C. to rank colleges in a new hierarchy and, having done so, to split off all lower-level work in the chosen institutions, thereby linking their future firmly to the new 'diploma in technology', the forerunner of the degrees awarded by the National Council for Academic Awards.

When the 1961 review of London's Further Education scheme was completed, there emerged three colleges of advanced technology, eight regional colleges also undertaking some advanced work, and eighteen area colleges concentrating mainly on lower-level work. Colleges of commerce were fitted into the same structure, but the art colleges remained in a separate category.

In addition, there were the local colleges based on the old day colleges and the technical and commercial institutes and forming thirteen colleges of further education, with a vital part to play as a link between vocational and non-vocational education. They are intended in principle for the boy or girl who is uncommitted to any career. Most have three departments – general, commercial and technical – and nearly all their students are under 18. Most of these colleges have developed special interests. Hackney has a lot of experience of dealing with young immigrants and Kingsway with the handicapped. Administratively London has found it difficult in practice to draw any firm line separating the work of the technical colleges from that of the colleges of further education. The original purpose of the thirteen colleges was to provide for the expected increase in the number of students released by their employers when day release was finally made compulsory, as a result of the influence of the Industrial Training Act. Day release has not become compulsory and the Industrial Training Act has so far not had the dramatic effect that some had expected. So in the past few years the number of day release students in colleges of further education has remained almost stationary while the number of full-time students has shot up. There has also been a tendency for more students over 18 to attend the colleges.

The unity of further education in London was one of the issues during the long controversy about the reorganization of local government in the Greater London area. The London colleges were serving a huge population drawn from the Greater London area. Any scheme for the redesign of the administrative map of London's education service had to take account of this. In the end, the survival of the Inner London Education Authority and free-trade agreements with neighbouring authorities have preserved the unity while at the same time maintaining the range of specialist and advanced colleges.

It would have been surprising if London had come to the end of its first century of public education without this Centenary coinciding with yet more reorganization in further education as five 'polytechnics' of the new style are struggling to be born. Each new polytechnic is based on a merger of two or more existing colleges, some of them 'aided' and including among their number such illustrious names as the Polytechnic, Regent Street, Sir John Cass College and the Brixton School of Building. Bringing them together into strong and independent colleges will be a major administrative task once the initial hurdles have been overcome.

They represent the jewels in London's higher education crown – standard bearers for the public sector in the binary controversy – but national institutions which happen to be based in London, rather than the expression of purely local endeavour. In this, of course, lies a vindication of all that Sidney Webb and the Technical Education Board stood for, with their clear-sighted recognition of London's metropolitan role in a national education policy. But the tensions are obvious enough. Scarcely a week passes without a suggestion that the polytechnics should sooner or later

188 Further and higher education

be elevated to the autonomous university sector, as if this were part of an evolutionary progression without which real merit cannot be achieved. The role of the polytechnic – combining full- and part-time higher education in a new and fruitful way, with a direct concern in relating educational needs to the working needs of society – still has to be filled out in practice. The challenge is still with the I.L.E.A. to show what London means by this new kind of institution, and how a great city can give the polytechnics practical support without inhibiting the development of new curricula and new methods. Equally, the colleges have to show that their ambition is to be themselves, not ape other institutions whose prestige is greater.

Select bibliography

BOARD OF EDUCATION, *New Code* (1890).

SCHOOL BOARD FOR LONDON, *Annual Reports.*
— *The Work of Three Years – School Board for London Report* (1870–73).
— *Report of Special Committee on Underfed Children* (1895).
— *Final Report of the School Board for London, 1870–1904* (2nd revised edn)
(1904).

SCHOOL BOARD FOR LONDON AND CITY AND GUILDS OF LONDON
TECHNICAL INSTITUTES, *Joint Committee on Manual Training* (vol. 1,
1887–90; vol. 2, 1891–3; vol. 3, 1894–5).

TECHNICAL EDUCATION BOARD, *Annual Reports* (1893–1902/3).

LONDON COUNTY COUNCIL, *Annual Reports* (1904–37).
— *Education in London* (vol. 1, 1945–54; vol. 2, 1954–7; vol. 3, 1957–62).
— *The Council's Jubilee as Local Education Authority: Report by the
Education Officer* (1954).
— *Report on Technical Education* (1892).
— *The Origin and Development of Central Schools* (1906).
— *Twenty-five Years of London Government* (1910–35); see pp. 17–25.
— *Eight Years of Technical Education and Continuation Schools* (1912).
— *The Evening School Reorganization Scheme* (1913).
— *Report of the Council to 31 March 1919.* (1920); see pp. 47–70.
— *The London Scheme of Further Education* (1944).
— *The London School Plan: A Development Plan for Primary and Secondary
Education* (1947).
— *Replanning London's Schools* (1947).
— *New Boarding Schools for London's Handicapped Children* (1951).
— *The Organization of Comprehensive Secondary Schools* (1954).
— *London Comprehensive Schools: A Survey of Sixteen Schools* (1961).

— *London Education Service* (1st edition published 1908) 12th edition (1961).
— *On From School: Educational Provision for Young People under the Age of 18 who have Left School* (1962).
— *Special Education in London* (1964) (see also I.L.E.A.).

INNER LONDON EDUCATION AUTHORITY, *Minutes of Proceedings of the Authority* (1964–).
— *Minutes of Proceedings of the Education Committee* (1964–).
— *Survey into the Progress of Maladjusted Pupils* (1965).
— *London Comprehensive Schools* (1966).
— *Special Education* (1968). (Originally published by the L.C.C. as *Special Education in London*, 1964.)

ROYAL COMMISSION ON LOCAL GOVERNMENT IN GREATER LONDON 1957–60, *Report* (1960).
ROYAL COMMISSION ON LOCAL GOVERNMENT IN ENGLAND 1966–9. Research studies:
— No. 2. The Greater London Group of the London School of Economics and Political Science (University of London).
Lessons of the London Government Reform (1968).
— No. 6. Research Unit on School Management and Government, University of London (Institute of Education).
School Management and Government (1968).
— No. 8. Tinker, A., *The Inner London Education Authority: A Study of Divisional Administration* (1968).

Acland, A., and Smith, H., *Studies of Secondary Education* (1892).
Allen, B. M., *Down the Stream of Life* (1948).
— *William Garnett – A Memoir* (1933).
Bayley, E., *Education in London Board Schools* (1888).
— *The Work of the School Board for London, 1888–1891* (1891).
Bourne, R., and MacArthur, B., *Struggle for Education*, a picture history of the N.U.T. (1970).
Burton, H. M., *There Was a Young Man* (1958).
Dent, H. C., *Education in Transition: A Sociological Study of the Impact of War on English Education 1939–1943* (1944).
— *Growth in English Education 1946–1952* (1954).
Department of Education and Science, *Education Act 1870*, a folder of facsimile documents relating to education in England and Wales and the passage of the 1870 Act (1970).
— *Trends in Education*, 1870 centenary issue (1970).
Gautrey, T., *Lux Mihi Laus: School Board Memories* (1937).

Gibbon, Sir G. and Bell, R., *A History of the L.C.C., 1889–1939* (1939).

Guest, L. H., *The New Education* (1920).

Hayward, F. H., *An Educational Failure: A School Inspector's Story* (1938).

Jackson, W. E., *Achievement: A Short History of the London County Council* (1965).

Jacob, W., 'London Secondary Technical Schools for Girls', *Journal of Education*, August 1954, p. 365.

Judges, A., *Education in Greater London* (1961).

Lindsay, K., *Social Progress and Educational Waste* (1926).

Lowndes, G. A. N., *Margaret McMillan, 'the Children's Champion'* (1960).

— *The Silent Social Revolution: An Account of Public Education in England and Wales, 1895–1965* (1st edn 1937; 2nd edn 1969).

Lubran, A., 'An Educational Experiment under Special Conditions of a Wartime Emergency School in London', *Practical Education and School Crafts*, May 1943.

Mais, S. P. B., *Fifty Years of the L.C.C.* (1939); see pp. 36–51.

Morley, C., *Studies in Board Schools* (1897).

Morley, R., *The Development in London of Elementary Education of a Higher Type: 1900–1910* (published privately by the author, 1961).

Morrish, I., *Education Since 1870* (1970).

Philpott, H. B., *London at School – The Story of the London School Board, 1870–1904* (1904).

Reid, J. W., *The Life of the Rt Hon. W. E. Forster* (1888, reprinted 1970).

Rhodes, G., *The Government of London: The Struggle for Reform* (1970).

Rich, E. E., *Education Act 1870* (1970).

Rubinstein, D., *School Attendance in London, 1870–1904* (1969).

Spalding, T. A. and Canney, T. S. A., *The Work of the London School Board* (1900).

Trevelyan, C. P., *The Cause of Children* (1897).

Webb, B., *Our Partnership* (1948).

Webb, S. J., *London Education* (1904).

Index